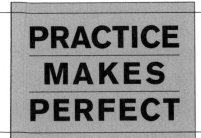

**PRACTICE
MAKES
PERFECT**

D0939624

Beginning Portuguese

with Two Audio CDs

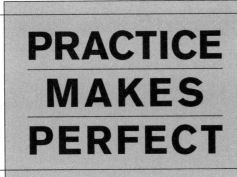

PRACTICE MAKES PERFECT

Beginning Portuguese
with Two Audio CDs

Sue Tyson-Ward

McGraw Hill

New York   Chicago   San Francisco   Lisbon   London   Madrid   Mexico City
Milan   New Delhi   San Juan   Seoul   Singapore   Sydney   Toronto

1 2 3 4 5 6 7 8 9 10 11 12 13 14 15   QDB/QDB   1 9 8 7 6 5 4 3 2 1

ISBN   978-0-07-175341-8 (book and CD-ROM set)
MHID   0-07-175341-9 (book and CD-ROM set)

ISBN   978-0-07-175338-8 (book for set)
MHID   0-07-175338-9 (book for set)

Library of Congress Control Number 2010936017

Trademarks: McGraw-Hill, the McGraw-Hill Publishing logo, Practice Makes Perfect, and related trade dress are trademarks or registered trademarks of The McGraw-Hill Companies and/or its affiliates in the United States and other countries and may not be used without written permission. All other trademarks are the property of their respective owners. The McGraw-Hill Companies is not associated with any product or vendor mentioned in this book.

First published in a different form as *Time for Portuguese*, by Stanley Thornes Ltd., Cheltenham, England, 1999.

McGraw-Hill books are available at special quantity discounts to use as premiums and sales promotions or for use in corporate training programs. To contact a representative, please e-mail us at bulksales@mcgraw-hill.com.

This book is printed on acid-free paper.

Contents

Introduction

Welcome to this new course, designed for beginners to the Portuguese language. Portuguese is now the world's sixth most spoken language, and it is a rapidly growing language of communication across the globe. It is the third most spoken European language in the world (after English and Spanish) and of course, already has a stronghold in South America due to the "giant" county of Brazil. It is also a very exciting language to embark on, given the potential of the cultural aspects you will also take on board; of a language which has touched not only Europe and Latin America, but also Africa, India, and the Far East. The Portuguese on the recordings is standard European, but we have indicated differences of vocabulary between Portugal and Brazil. You will still go far in Brazil, even with European Portuguese, once you tune your ear to the different sounds the Brazilians make. After all, it is really just akin to the differences between American and British English.

The material in this course has been designed for you to complete one unit every day, but you are in control. If you want to cover several units in a day, then do that. Do try, however, to stick to a sensible routine so that you cover a number of units spread over the course of one week, rather than ten sessions on the weekend. You will retain so much more if you "drip-feed" yourself. You should ideally work through the units in sequence, but again, you are in control. Choose a method which suits you best. The topics of the course are cyclical in structure: there are 12 main themes which are repeated five times over the course. Each subsequent time you come to that theme, you will review what you learned in the previous cycle and then progress further with it.

Start by reading the **Vocabulário** (*vocabulary*) section. Then listen to the **Diálogo** (*dialogue*) section, first of all without following the transcript in the book, and then using the text. This uses the words on the word list you have already been practicing. See how much you can understand before you consult the text. Don't worry if there are parts you miss—just try to catch the drift of what is said, or simply listen to the sound and intonation of the language, as spoken by our native speakers.

We use the following symbols in the course:

m.	masculine word
f.	feminine word
pl.	plural
BP	Brazilian Portuguese term
EP	European Portuguese reference

The spellings throughout this course adhere to the latest Portuguese Spelling Agreement, which came into effect in 2007.

Once you have read through the text and unravelled its contents, you are ready for the *exercises* (**Atividades**). Some of these involve the recording, some don't. In Exercise 3 of every unit you will be asked to take part in a speaking activity. Usually this takes the form of a dialogue with an actor on the recording. You will be given prompts in English on the recording for the first 12 units. These dialogues are also written in the book, and you will hear the correct version after the pause on the recording. Make sure you follow the sequence of these prompts carefully to guide you in your responses. You will soon get used to the method used here, and you will find it invaluable in gaining confidence in speaking naturally.

All the answers to the **Atividades** are in the back of the book, where you will also find a brief summary of the grammar covered in the course, and a basic vocabulary list.

The **Língua** section explains some of the structures which may have arisen in the dialogue, and you can tackle this before you try out the exercises. The **De interesse** sections give you some background on the culture and lifestyle of Portugal and Brazil.

Do come back to units in the future to refresh your memory. Once you have covered the unit with the help of the book, you will find that playing the recordings in your car, or wherever, will prove invaluable.

Good luck and enjoy learning Portuguese! **Boa sorte!**

Pronunciation guide

Here is a simple guide to the letters of the alphabet, with their Portuguese names and how to pronounce the names:

A	á	*ah*
B	bê	*bay*
C	cê	*say*
D	dê	*day*
E	é	*eh*
F	efe	*eff*
G	guê	*gay*
H	agá	*ah-gah*
I	i	*ee*
J	jota	*zhoh-tah*
K	capa	*cah-pah*
L	ele	*el*
M	eme	*em*
N	ene	*en*
O	ó	*oh*
P	pê	*pay*
Q	quê	*kay*
R	erre	*air*
S	esse	*ess*
T	tê	*tay*
U	u	*oo*
V	vê	*vay*
W	double vê *or* dáblio	*double vay/double-u*, almost like the English *w*
X	xis	*shish*
Y	ípsilon *or* i grego	*eepsilon* or *ee-graygoo*
Z	zê	*zay*

Less familiar sounds

Most Portuguese words are pronounced as they are written. Once you have decoded a few tricky sounds, you should be able to have a go at reading Portuguese aloud as you see it. Here are some basic guidelines for some of the trickier sounds:

ch	*sh*
lh	like the *lli* in *billion*

nh	like the *ni* in on*i*on
g, followed by **e/i**	like the *s* in plea*s*ure
j	as above
h	always silent
x	tricky—varies from hard *ks* sound to a z, or even *sh*.

Nasal sounds

Nasal sounds pronounced at the back of the nose are indicated by a ~ (tilde) over the vowel, and they also include words ending in -**m** or -**n**.

ão	*ow*
ãos	*owsh*
õe	*oy*
ões	*oysh*
ã	*ah*
ãs	*ahsh*
ãe	*eye*
ães	*eyesh*

One thing to remember is that when words run together when spoken, there is an effect on the ending and beginning of words involved, which may alter the sound from when a word is spoken in isolation from others.

c, g, and **q**

A quick note here about the consonants **c**, **g**, and **q**, which change their pronunciation depending on which vowels follow them.

c before **a/o/u**	→ hard sound, like *cap*
ç before **a/o/u**	→ soft sound, like *face*
c before **e/i**	→ soft
g before **e/i**	→ soft, like the *s* sound in *treasure*
g before **a/o/u**	→ hard, like in *goat*
g + u before **e/i**	→ silent *u*; for example, **guitarra** is pronounced *ghee,* not *gwee*
qu before **e/i**	→ silent *u*; for example, **máquina** (*machine*) is pronounced *mákeena,* not *mákweena*

There are some exceptions:

linguiça (spicy sausage)	→ *lingwiça*
qu before *o/a*	→ *kw*; for example, **quadro** (*picture*) is pronounced *kwadro*

Ph does not exist in Portuguese. Those words similar to English have an *f*—the same sound, but be careful with the spelling; for example, **filósofo** (*philosopher*).

Brazilian spelling

The new **Acordo Ortográfico** (*spelling agreement*), in circulation since 2007, has aimed to standardize a lot of spelling across the Portuguese-speaking world, although there are still some differences between the two main variants of the language, Brazilian and Luso-African it includes that which is spoken in Portugal and also those African countries with Portuguese as an official language. Changes that have been agreed upon will still take a number of years to implement in all written material. This course complies with the new Acordo.

Stress (emphasis)

Portuguese words fall into three groups in terms of where the stress (emphasis) falls when a word is spoken:

- last syllable
- penultimate (next to last)
- antepenultimate (two syllables from the end)

Most words belong to the second group. A written accent is put on the word to enable them to be correctly stressed when they have deviated from the usual stress-pattern. Whenever you see a written accent, that is where you should emphasize the word when you say it. You will come across the following written accents:

- ` grave accent
- ´ acute accent
- ^ circumflex accent
- ~ tilde—also a sign of a nasal sound

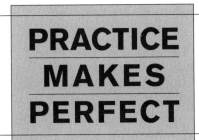

PRACTICE MAKES PERFECT

Beginning Portuguese

with Two Audio CDs

People

Introductions

VOCABULÁRIO (*vocabulary*)

bem-vinda [f.] (a)	*welcome (to)*
Bom dia.	*Hello. Good morning.*
Chamo-me . . . ;	*My name is . . .*
[BP] Eu me chamo . . .	
Como se chama?	*What's your name?*
De onde é?	*Where are you from?*
igualmente	*likewise*
Inglaterra [f.]	*England*
muito bem	*very well; well then*
Muito prazer.	*Pleased to meet you.*
no norte	*in the north*
Obrigada. [f.]	*Thank you.*
sou (de)	*I am (from)*
Sou inglês.	*I am English. (an English man)*
Sou inglesa.	*I am English. (an English woman)*

Diálogo (*dialogue*)

ANNE: Bom dia, sou Anne Green. Como se chama o senhor?

ANTÓNIO: Chamo-me António da Silva.

ANNE: Muito prazer.

ANTÓNIO: Igualmente. De onde é, Anne?

ANNE: Sou inglesa. Sou de Manchester, no norte da Inglaterra.

ANTÓNIO: Muito bem. Bem-vinda a Portugal, Anne.

ANNE: Obrigada.

Fill in the following speech bubbles as if you are the person, giving your name and the town you come from. The first one is an example for you.

1. Lisboa — Chamo-me Pedro. Sou de Lisboa. — Pedro

2. Paris — Françoise

3. Londres — Mark

4. Berlim — Helga

ATIVIDADE

1·2

Listen to the recording of three people saying who they are and where they are from in Portugal. Fill in their details on the table below.

NAME	FROM
1. _____	_____
2. _____	_____
3. _____	_____

ATIVIDADE 1·3

Now take part in a dialogue using the English prompts below to guide you.

1. Good morning, my name is Frank.

2. I am English; I am from Lancaster.

3. I am pleased to meet you too.

Língua (language)

You do not necessarily need to use the word for *I* (**eu**), as the verb forms demonstrate who is speaking: **Sou**, *(I) am;* **chamo**, *(I) am called.*

> In Brazil, it is more usual to say **me chamo** than **chamo-me**. You can also say **meu nome é . . .** *(my name is . . .).*

Adjectives (words of description), such as for nationality, have different forms for male (masculine) and female (feminine). Usually the male form ends in **-o**, and the female in **-a**.

americano	*American man*
americana	*American woman*

There are exceptions to spelling. You will see there is no **o** on the male form here:

inglês	*English (man)*
inglesa	*English (woman)*

These changes also apply to other words:

bem-vindo	*welcome (to a male)*
bem-vinda	*welcome (to a female)*
obrigado	*thank you (said by a male)*
obrigada	*thank you (said by a female)*

De interesse (of interest)

There are many ways of saying *you* in Portuguese, depending on how formal you are being. The Portuguese people show respect when talking to strangers, older people, or those in a superior (work or social) position. For most of your dealings you will hear/use **o senhor/a senhora** (literally, *the gentleman/the lady*) or simply the verb without the word for *you*, as in **De onde é?** (literally, *From where are [you]?*).

> In Brazil, most people call each other **você** *(you).*

·2· Eating out
Snacks and drinks

VOCABULÁRIO	
água mineral [f.]	*mineral water*
Boa tarde.	*Hello. Good afternoon.*
café [m.]; [BP] um cafezinho	*small black coffee*
com gás	*fizzy*
Diga?	*Can I help you? [lit. "say" (what you want)]*
e	*and*
empada de galinha [f.]	*small chicken pie*
Faz favor!	*Please!/Excuse me! (said to grab a waiter's attention)*
fresca [f.]	*chilled*
Mais alguma coisa?	*Anything else?*
não	*no*
natural	*at room temperature*
ou	*or*
pastel de nata [m.]	*custard cake*
queria	*I would like*
se faz favor; [BP/EP] por favor	*please/if you please*
sem gás	*still (not fizzy)*
sim	*yes*
um [m.]	*a/one*
uma [f.]	*a/one*

Diálogo

CUSTOMER: Faz favor!

WAITER: Boa tarde. Diga, se faz favor.

CUSTOMER: Queria um café e uma água mineral sem gás.

WAITER: Fresca ou natural?

CUSTOMER: Fresca, se faz favor.

WAITER: Mais alguma coisa?

CUSTOMER: Sim, um pastel de nata e uma empada de galinha. Obrigada.

WAITER: Obrigado.

ATIVIDADE 2·1

Fill in the blanks in these sentences according to the pictures.

1. Queria_____, se faz favor.

2. Queria_____, por favor.

3. Queria_____ e _____, se faz favor.

ATIVIDADE 2·2

Listen to the recording of two people ordering snacks and drinks from a café. Mark the appropriate category with details of what they order in the table below.

UM CAFÉ	UMA ÁGUA MINERAL	UM PASTEL DE NATA	UMA EMPADA
1. _____	_____	_____	_____
2. _____	_____	_____	_____

ATIVIDADE 2·3

Now take part in a dialogue using the English prompts to guide you.

1. I would like a chicken pie.

2. Yes, I would like a mineral water, please.

3. Chilled.

4. Fizzy.

Língua

All nouns (objects, people, abstract ideas) in Portuguese are divided into masculine and feminine words. Usually words ending in **-o** are masculine, and those in **-a** are feminine.

Masculine		Feminine	
um bolo	*a cake*	**uma água**	*a water*

There are many exceptions to this endings rule, so be prepared to learn them as you go along. For example:

um café	*a coffee*
um pastel	*a cake, pastry*

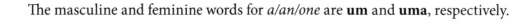

The masculine and feminine words for *a/an/one* are **um** and **uma**, respectively.

De interesse

There is a great variety of coffees in Portugal and Brazil—catering to every imaginable need. You could ask for **um café** (**uma bica** in Lisbon) for a small, espresso-style black coffee, known as a **cafezinho** in Brazil; **um galão** for a very milky coffee served in a glass in Portugal. There is also **um pingado**—a small, black coffee with one drop of milk; **uma italiana**—a very strong espresso; **uma meia de leite** or **um café com leite**—white coffee in a normal sized cup, which is the term also used in Brazil for the milky coffee consumed at breakfast.

Accommodations

Booking a room in a hotel

VOCABULÁRIO

Boa noite.	*Hello; Good evening.*
Está bem.	*Right then; OK.*
Para quantas pessoas?	*For how many people?*
Para quantas noites?	*For how many nights?*
para	*for*
quarto [m.]; [BP] um apartamento	*room*
quartos individuais	*single rooms*
quartos [pl.]	*rooms*
Querem . . . ?	*Do you (pl.) want . . . ?*
queríamos	*we would like*
Têm . . . ?	*Do you (pl.) have . . . ?*
temos	*we have*
um quarto de casal	*a double room*
um quarto individual	*a single room*
vagos [pl.]	*vacant/free*
um/uma	*one, a/an*
dois/duas	*two*
três	*three*
quatro	*four*
cinco	*five*
seis	*six*
sete	*seven*
oito	*eight*
nove	*nine*
dez	*ten*

Diálogo

CUSTOMER: Boa noite. Têm quartos vagos?

RECEPTIONIST: Boa noite senhora; sim, temos. Para quantas pessoas?

CUSTOMER: Para três.

RECEPTIONIST: Querem quartos individuais?

CUSTOMER: Não. Queríamos um quarto de casal, e um individual.

RECEPTIONIST: É para quantas noites?

CUSTOMER: Para cinco.

RECEPTIONIST: Está bem. Temos os quartos nove e seis.

Match the guests to their rooms by drawing a line to the appropriate picture.

1. Queria um quarto individual.

a.

2. Queríamos um quarto de casal.

b.

3. Queríamos dois quartos individuais.

c.

Listen to the recording of two people asking for hotel rooms and fill in the table below according to their requirements.

NUMBER OF PEOPLE	NUMBER OF NIGHTS	SINGLE ROOM(S)	DOUBLE ROOM(S)
1. _____	_____	_____	_____
2. _____	_____	_____	_____

ATIVIDADE
3·3

Now take part in a dialogue using the English prompts on the recording and in your book to guide you.

1. Good morning. Do you have any rooms free?

2. For one.

3. For five.

Língua

The numbers *one* and *two* have two forms: masculine and feminine.

Masculine		Feminine	
um	*one*	**uma**	*one*
dois	*two*	**duas**	*two*

These are also the words for *a/an* as you saw in Unit 2.

Your choice of form depends on whether the object following the number is masculine or feminine, thus:

um quarto	*one/a room*
uma noite	*one/a night*
dois quartos	*two rooms*
duas pessoas	*two people*

You will also find in the dialogue some plural forms of words. Usually the plural (i.e., when there is more than one) is formed by simply adding an **-s** to a word, although there are exceptions.

Singular		Plural	
um quarto	*one room*	**um quarto individual**	*one single room*
cinco quartos	*five rooms*	**três quartos individuais**	*three single rooms*

De interesse

There are several ways of specifying your hotel room. A single room, as in our dialogue, is **um quarto individual** or **um quarto simples**. In Brazil, people usually request **um apartamento**, which sounds rather grand but is really just a room with its own bathroom. A **quarto** is often just a room, sharing communal washrooms. A double room can be **um quarto de casal** or **um quarto duplo**. Usually a double room will have two single beds in it (**com duas camas**). If you specifically want a double bed, you may have to request **com cama de casal**.

Travel

A bus journey

VOCABULÁRIO	
autocarro [m.]; [BP] o ônibus	*bus*
bilhetes [pl.]	*tickets*
de ida e volta	*return*
de ida	*single*
desculpe	*excuse me*
é, sim	*yes, it is*
Este é . . . ?	*Is this . . ./This is . . . ?*
minutos [m., pl.]	*minutes*
não, não é	*no, it's not*
Quanto tempo leva?	*How long does it take?*
só	*only*
um bilhete	*a ticket*
onze	11
doze	12
treze	13
catorze; [BP] *also* quatorze	14
quinze	15
dezasseis; [BP] dezesseis	16
dezassete; [BP] dezessete	17
dezoito	18
dezanove; [BP] dezenove	19
vinte	20

Diálogo

WOMAN: Este é o autocarro para Faro?

BUS DRIVER 1: Não, não é.

WOMAN: Desculpe, este é o autocarro para Faro?

BUS DRIVER 2: É, sim.

WOMAN: Queria dois bilhetes, se faz favor.

DRIVER 2: De ida, ou de ida e volta?

WOMAN: De ida e volta. Quanto tempo leva?

DRIVER 2: Só quinze minutos.

WOMAN: Obrigada.

Respond to the questions below as if you were the driver of each bus, writing your answer in the space provided. We have answered the first for you.

1. Este é o autocarro para Lisboa?   *É, sim.*

2. Este é o autocarro para Faro?   _____

3. Este é o ônibus para Brasília?   _____

4. Este é o autocarro para Silves?   _____

*Listen to the three people on the recording, asking for tickets to different destinations. Then decide whether the following statements are true (**verdadeiro**) or false (**falso**).*

WANTS	TO	V	F
1. Return ticket	Carvoeiro	_____	_____
2. 2 single tickets	Évora	_____	_____
3. 2 returns	Fátima	_____	_____

Three people will ask you about journey times. Use the information below and tell them how long each trip takes.

1. To Lisboa   17 minutes

2. To Faro   13 minutes

3. To Estoril   19 minutes

Língua

You can work out a pattern to help learn the numbers in Portuguese. Look at numbers 11–15: They all have the same ending (-**ze**), and the English word *dozen* may help you to remember the number 12. Numbers 16–19 are based on the 10 plus the last digit, thus 17 = **dez as sete**.

There are four variations for the word *the* in Portuguese: **o/a/os/as**.

	Singular	Plural
Masculine	o autocarro	os bilhetes
Feminine	a pessoa	as noites

De interesse

If you are traveling by bus within a city or its close boundaries in Portugal, you can buy a book of prepaid tickets (often called **módulos**, or a **caderneta**), which are cheaper than individual tickets. As you enter the bus, you "click" the ticket in a small clipper machine. On many urban buses in Brazil, you enter the vehicle at the back, go through a turnstyle operated by a ticket collector, where you pay, and then get off at the front.

Directions

Getting to the tourist office

VOCABULÁRIO	
à direita	*right, on/to the right*
à esquerda	*left, on/to the left*
a pé	*on foot*
aqui	*here*
claro	*of course*
da praça	*of the square*
de nada	*don't mention it*
do lado direito	*on the right-hand side*
do lado esquerdo	*on the left-hand side*
fica	*it is (situated)*
há; há? ; [BP] *also uses* tem	*there is/are; is/are there?*
longe	*far*
mais devagar	*more slowly*
na praça	*in the square*
perto	*near*
Pode repetir?	*Can you repeat (it)?*
segue em frente	*(you) carry straight ahead*
um posto de turismo	*a tourist office*
vira	*(you) turn*

Diálogo

VISITOR: Desculpe, há um posto de turismo aqui?

WOMAN: Sim, há um na praça de São Jorge.

VISITOR: Fica muito longe?

WOMAN: Não, fica perto. O senhor vira aqui à esquerda, segue em frente, e o turismo fica do lado direito da praça.

VISITOR: Desculpe, pode repetir mais devagar se faz favor.

WOMAN: Claro. O senhor vira aqui à esquerda, segue em frente, e o turismo fica do lado direito da praça. Leva só dez minutos a pé.

VISITOR: Muito obrigado.

WOMAN: De nada.

à esquerda   em frente   à direita

Indicate whether the directions with each map will lead you to the tourist office underlining **sim** *(yes) or* **não** *(no).*

1.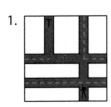

O senhor segue em frente, vira à esquerda, vira à direita, e o turismo fica em frente.

sim ou **não**

2.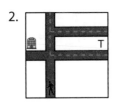

O senhor segue em frente, vira à esquerda, e o turismo fica à direita.

sim ou **não**

Listen to someone on the recording receiving directions to the tourist office and note in English the information they are given on the table below. Listen to the whole exercise before taking notes.

FIRST	THEN	NEXT (2 INSTRUCTIONS)	THEN	WHERE IS THE OFFICE?

Now take part in a dialogue yourself, using the English prompts to help you and speaking in the pauses in the recording.

1. Excuse me, is there a tourist office here?

2. Is it very far?

3. Can you repeat it a bit slower please?

4. Thank you.

Língua

In the dialogue you came across the expressions **na praça** (*in the square*) and **da praça** (*of the square*). These forms have come from a combination of words, contracted to ease pronunciation. It is the words for *the* combining with the words for *in* (**em**) and *of* (**de**):

	+o	+a	+os	+as	*the*
em (*in/on*)	**no**	**na**	**nos**	**nas**	*in/on the*
de (*of/from*)	**do**	**da**	**dos**	**das**	*of/from the*

You will find other contracted words as you work through the course.

De interesse

Most Portuguese people do speak rather quickly, and you may experience some trouble understanding their initial responses to your questions. It is particularly awkward in the Algarve, where they tend to chop off the beginnings and endings of words; thus the words **vinho tinto** (*red wine*) may sound like **vin tint**. Brazilians tend to speak with more open vowel sounds, thus making it slightly easier to follow what they are saying.

Town amenities

At the tourist office

VOCABULÁRIO	
aqui está	*here you are/here is*
aqui tem	*here you have*
às quintas [f., pl.]	*on Thursdays*
às terças [f., pl.]	*on Tuesdays*
cidade [f.]	*city, town*
com certeza	*certainly*
excursão [f.]	*trip*
excursões [f., pl.]	*trips, excursions*
fazer	*to make, do*
folheto [m.]	*leaflet*
hotéis [m., pl.]	*hotels*
hotel [m.]	*hotel*
informações [f., pl.]	*information*
lá	*there*
lista [f.]	*list*
onde	*where*
pode	*you (he, she, it) can*
Posso . . . ?	*May/Can I . . . ?*
quando	*when*
reservas [f., pl.]	*reservations*
sobre	*about, on*
visitar	*to visit*
(a) segunda(-feira)*	*Monday*
(a) terça(-feira)	*Tuesday*
(a) quarta(-feira)	*Wednesday*
(a) quinta(-feira)	*Thursday*
(a) sexta(-feira)	*Friday*
(o) sábado	*Saturday*
(o) domingo	*Sunday*

* Lit. second (day), etc.

Diálogo

VISITOR: Boa tarde. Têm informações sobre Lisboa?

TOURISM AGENT: Temos, sim. Aqui tem um folheto sobre a cidade, e uma lista de hotéis.

VISITOR: Posso fazer reservas para excursões aqui?

AGENT: Pode, sim. Para onde?

VISITOR: Queria visitar Évora. Quando há excursões para lá?

AGENT: Há excursões às terças e às quintas.

VISITOR: Bom, queria um bilhete para a quinta-feira, se faz favor.

AGENT: Com certeza. Aqui está.

ATIVIDADE 6·1

Match the English statements to what people are saying in Portuguese.

1. Sylvia wants a list of hotels and a trip to Faro for Saturday.

2. John wants a leaflet about Salvador, a trip to Olinda on Sunday, and a list of hotels.

3. Frank wants a trip to Faro for Wednesday, a leaflet on Oporto, and an excursion to Nazaré on Monday.

a. Queria um folheto sobre o Porto, um bilhete para Faro para a quarta-feira, e um bilhete para a Nazaré, para a segunda-feira.

c. Queria uma lista de hotéis e um bilhete para Faro para sábado.

b. Queria um bilhete para Olinda, para domingo, uma lista de hotéis e um folheto sobre Salvador.

d. Queria um bilhete para Olinda para quinta-feira e uma lista de hotéis.

ATIVIDADE 6·2

Listen to two people on the recording booking excursions at a tourist office, and fill in the table below according to the reservations they make.

EXCURSION TO?	WHICH DAY?
1. _____	_____
2. _____	_____

Now try re-creating the dialogue using the prompts on the recording to guide you.

1. Good morning.

2. Do you have information on Oporto?

3. Can I book excursions here?

4. To Fátima.

5. I would like two tickets for Wednesday.

Língua

There are a few examples in the dialogue of words in the plural, which do not belong to the simple + **s** formation we saw in Unit 3.

Ending	Singular		Plural	
+ ão	a excursão	*trip*	as excursões	*trips*
	a informação	*information*	as informações	*information (plural form more common)*
+ l	o hotel	*hotel*	os hotéis	*hotels*

Unfortunately, there are many exceptions to the rules, so learn irregular words as you go along.

De interesse

The *days of the week* (**os dias da semana**) in Portuguese are mostly unlike those in the other Latin-based languages, apart from the two days of the weekend. Since Monday begins as the *second* (**segunda**) day followed by the *third* (**terça**), you can count through up to the *fifth day* (**sexta**). In practice, the **feira** part of the expression of the day is dropped in spoken Portuguese; most people simply refer to **segunda**, **quinta**, etc.

Downtown

Where can I . . . ?

VOCABULÁRIO

ao pé de	*right next to*
banco [m.]	*bank*
bem	*well, well then*
carne [f.]	*meat*
comprar	*to buy*
farmácia [f.]	*chemist's, pharmacist's*
livraria [f.]	*bookshop*
livro [m.]	*book*
mandar consertar	*to have mended (to mend)*
mercearia [f.]	*grocer's*
na esquina [f.]	*on the corner*
obrigadinha [f.]	*thanks very much*
Onde é que . . . ?	*Where (is it that) . . . ?*
outra coisa [f.]	*another thing*
padaria [f.]	*bakery*
pão [m.]	*bread*
Pois . . .	*Well, er . . .*
sapateiro [m.]	*shoe mender*
sapatos [m., pl.]	*shoes*
talho [m.]; [BP] o açougue	*butchers*

🔘 Diálogo

WOMAN: Desculpe, onde é que posso comprar pão?

MAN: Pão? Pois, há uma padaria na esquina.

WOMAN: Obrigada. Ah—outra coisa, (er), onde é que posso mandar consertar os sapatos?

MAN: Os sapatos? Bem, há um sapateiro na praça, ao pé do banco.

WOMAN: Obrigadinha.

MAN: De nada. Bom dia.

Draw a line from the pictures to place the items in the correct shops.

1.   a. o talho/o açougue

2.   b. a livraria

3.   c. a farmácia

4.   d. o sapateiro

5.   e. a padaria

Listen to two people asking where they can buy various items, and write down where they are sent.

1. Speaker 1 _____

2. Speaker 2 _____

Now it's your turn to take part in a dialogue. Follow the prompts and speak in the pauses.

1. Excuse me, where can I buy a book?

2. Thank you. Ah, another thing—where can I buy some meat?

3. Thanks very much.

Língua

In Unit 3, you learned that the numeral *one* (**um, uma**) was also the word for *a/an*, and that it had both a masculine and feminine form. We can see it being used in the dialogue opposite, in **uma padaria** (*a baker's*) and **um sapateiro** (*a cobbler's*). The plural forms of these words, which correspond to the English *some* are **uns** (m., pl.) and **umas** (f., pl.), thus:

> **uns jornais** = *some newspapers*
> **umas laranjas** = *some oranges*

In practice, however, you will find that the word for *some* is often omitted in most conversational situations.

> **Queria comprar jornais.**   *I would like to buy [some] newspapers.*

De interesse

The word **pois** is the Portuguese equivalent of saying *er* or *well*. It is extremely common and is a useful prop if you can't immediately find your next word. Brazilians find it rather amusing and typical of their European cousins. They tend to use expressions such as:

tá (from **está**)	*right/OK*
então	*so/then*
né? (from **não é**)	*isn't it/right/yeah*

The form of **obrigado**, which is in the dialogue as **obrigadinha**, is known as a diminutive (or smaller) form. Again, this is very common as it is considered friendlier. Remember, if you are a man you would say **obrigadinho**. Listen out for these **-inho** forms when you are in Portugal or Brazil.

Personal choices

Likes and dislikes

┌─ **VOCABULÁRIO** ─────────────────────────────────┐

acho (que)	*I think (that)*
cara [f.]	*expensive*
comércio [m.]	*business*
então	*well (then)*
Eu	*I*
Gosta (de) . . . ?	*Do you like . . . ?*
gosto	*I (do) like*
igreja [f.]	*church*
mais	*more*
mas	*but*
menos	*less*
muito (muitos)	*a lot, much (many)*
não muito	*not much*
Olá; [BP] Oi	*Hi, hello there*
pessoalmente	*personally*
porque	*because*
prefiro	*I prefer*
também	*also*
trânsito [m.]	*traffic*
ver	*to see*

└───┘

Diálogo

Woman: Olá, João, bom dia. Então, gosta de Lisboa?

Man: Gosto, sim. Há muito para fazer.

Woman: Eu também gosto, mas acho que prefiro Coimbra—há menos trânsito. O João gosta de Coimbra?

Man: Gosto, mas não muito. Pessoalmente, prefiro o Porto porque há mais comércio.

Woman: E Braga? Gosta?

Man: Gosto muito. Há muitas igrejas para ver.

Look at what the following people are saying about various places, and decide which of the cities they would prefer to be in.

1.
> Gosto de Londres e Paris, mas prefiro Madrid.

4.
> Não gosto de Manaus. Prefiro Paris porque há muito para ver.

2.
> Gosto muito de Lisboa. Não gosto de Madrid-é muito cara.

5.
> Gosto de Madrid, mas não gosto muito de Lisboa. Pessoalmente gosto mais de Londres.

3.
> Não gosto muito de Londres-há muito trânsito, mas gosto de Manaus.

a. Lisboa

b. Paris

c. Londres

d. Madrid

e. Manaus

Listen to José and Ana talking about which cities they like and dislike, and mark their responses on the table.

	JOSÉ		ANA	
	gosta	não gosta	gosta	não gosta
Braga	_____	_____	_____	_____
Lisboa	_____	_____	_____	_____
Albufeira	_____	_____	_____	_____
Porto	_____	_____	_____	_____

Now take part in an interview about your likes and dislikes of various cities. Follow the prompts on the recording to guide you.

1. I like it very much. There is a lot to see.

2. No, I don't like Paris very much.

3. Yes, I prefer Madrid because there is a lot to do.

Língua

In the dialogue we found the word **muito** used for three very different meanings:

há muito para fazer	*a lot of things (there is a lot to do)*
gosto muito	*much (I like much/a lot)*
há muitas igrejas	*many (there are many churches)*

Note that when **muito** means *much* or *many*, when used with a noun, its ending will change (m./f./pl.) according to the noun that follows it:

muito tempo	*much (a lot of) time*
muitos livros	*many books*
muita água	*much (a lot of) water*
muitas pessoas	*many people*

De interesse

There is a Portuguese saying about the main cities in Portugal: **Coimbra canta, Braga reza, Lisboa desfila e o Porto trabalha** (*Coimbra sings, Braga prays, Lisbon parades and o Porto works*), referring to distinct characteristics of those cities.

Vacations

Discussing your holiday

VOCABULÁRIO	
(de) primavera [f.]	*(of) spring*
a Capela dos Ossos	*the Chapel of Bones (see De interesse)*
adoro	*I love*
agora	*now*
amendoeiras [f., pl.]	*almond trees*
boas férias [f., pl.]	*good holiday(s)*
bonito	*pretty*
cá	*here*
castelo [m.]	*castle*
de férias	*on vacation, on holiday*
de negócios	*on business*
é verdade	*that's true*
é	*is (also you are, formal)*
está	*you are (formal/polite); also: he, she, it is*
estão	*are (plural)*
estou	*I am*
faz calor	*it is hot*
outra vez	*again*
passar	*to spend (time)*
pretendo	*I intend*
tanto	*so (much)/too*

Diálogo

MAN: Olá , Joana. Está cá outra vez?

WOMAN: Estou, sim. Gosto muito de Portugal.

MAN: Mas, está aqui de férias, ou de negócios?

WOMAN: De férias. Adoro passar as férias de primavera em Portugal, porque é muito bonito, e não faz tanto calor.

MAN: É verdade—no Algarve as amendoeiras estão muito bonitas agora.

WOMAN: Pretendo visitar Évora e ver a Capela dos Ossos.

MAN: Então, boas férias!

ATIVIDADE 9·1

*Fill in the blanks in this exercise with either **é** (is) or **são** (are), and make the describing adjective agree (match) with the object(s) in the pictures. Follow the example of number 1.*

1. **bonito**

   A Luisa *é* bonit *a*.

2. **pequeno** (*small*)

   O hotel __ pequen__.

3. **bonito**

   Os sapatos __ bonit__.

4. **barato** (*cheap*)

   As laranjas __ barat__.

5. **caro**

   A camisa __ car__.

ATIVIDADE 9·2

Listen to Joana and Mr. Oliveira talking about their holidays, and fill in the blanks in the dialogue below.

JOANA _____ Sr. Oliveira. Está _____ de _____ ou de _____?

SR. OLIVEIRA De _____ Adoro passar _____ em Portugal porque _____

bonito e _____ é muito _____.

JOANA Sim, agora as cidades _____ muito _____.

SR. OLIVEIRA Pois, pretendo _____ Lisboa e _____ o castelo de São Jorge.

JOANA _____, boas férias!

ATIVIDADE
9·3

Now join in a dialogue based on the previous one. You will be prompted in English on the recording. If you feel like stretching yourself, you can give your own reasons for liking places.

1. Yes, I am. I like Portugal very much.

2. I'm on holiday, because it's not too hot and it's very pretty.

3. I intend to visit Évora.

Língua

By now, you have come across two different ways of saying *you are* (**é/está**) and *I am* (**sou/estou**). This is because Portuguese has two verbs *to be*: **ser** and **estar**. **Ser** is used mainly for permanent things and characteristics, people's origins, and their nationality and profession. **Estar** is used mostly for temporary positions, locations, and states. Here is the present tense of the two verbs in full:

	I am	*you are (fam.)*	*he/she/it is* *you are (polite)*	*we are*	*they are* *you are (pl.)*
ser	sou	és	é	somos	são
estar	estou	estás	está	estamos	estão

Sou inglês.	*I am English.* (permanent characteristic/nationality)
Estou aqui de férias.	*I am here on vacation.* (temporary situation)

Note also that there is both a polite and a familiar way of addressing someone as *you*: **o senhor/a senhora** and **tu**, respectively. In Brazil, **tu** is rarely used; **você** is the norm, which takes the same verb form as the "polite" *you* (and *he/she/it*).

De interesse

A Capela dos Ossos is a chapel with walls completely covered with bones and skulls. There are two such macabre chapels in Portugal—one in Évora and another in Faro. If you intend to enter them or any religious building in Portugal or Brazil, you should wear appropriate clothing or you may be refused entry.

The weather

Talking about good weather

Ainda bem!	*Thank goodness!*
azul	*blue*
céu [m.]	*sky*
de laranja	*(of) orange*
de morango	*(of) strawberry*
gelados [m., pl.]; [BP] **sorvetes**	*ice creams*
hoje	*today*
não é?; [BP] *often* **né?**	*haven't we/isn't it?*
nuvem [f.]	*cloud*
nuvens [f., pl.]	*clouds*
que!	*what/what a!*
sorvetes [m., pl.]; [BP] **picolés**	*popsicles, ice lollies*
tempo [m.]	*weather*
tenho	*I have*
vento [m.]	*wind*

Diálogo

ICE CREAM VENDOR: Gelados! Gelados!

WOMAN: Ainda bem! Três gelados, se faz favor.

ICE CREAM VENDOR: Tenho gelados de morango e sorvetes de laranja e de morango.

WOMAN: Bom, então dois sorvetes de laranja, e um gelado.

ICE CREAM VENDOR: Muito bem. Que bom tempo temos, não é?

WOMAN: Sim, faz muito calor e não há vento.

ICE CREAM VENDOR: O céu está azul, e não há nuvens—está um dia bonito hoje.

Match the pictures with the weather descriptions.

1.   a. Faz bom tempo.

2.   b. Não há nuvens.

3.   c. Faz muito calor.

4.   d. Há vento.

5.   e. Há nuvens.

Listen to the following weather forecast for three Portuguese cities, and mark the table with a check mark, according to what you hear.

	BOM TEMPO	MUITO CALOR	CÉU AZUL	VENTO	NUVENS
Guarda	_____	_____	_____	_____	_____
Lisboa	_____	_____	_____	_____	_____
Setúbal	_____	_____	_____	_____	_____

Now take part in a dialogue based on the previous one. Follow the English prompts, and speak in the pauses on the recording.

1. Thank goodness! I'd like five ice creams, please.

2. Three strawberry (popsicles) ice lollies and two ice creams.

3. Yes, the sky is blue and there is no wind.

Língua

To talk about the weather, Portuguese uses a few different verbs, as you saw in the dialogue. Note the following:

fazer	*to do, make*
Faz calor.	***It is** hot.*
Faz bom tempo.	***It is** good weather.*
haver	*to have/be*
Há vento.	***It is** windy.*
Há nuvens.	***It is** cloudy.*
ter	*to have*
Temos bom tempo.	***We have** nice weather.*
Tem sol.	***There is** sun.*
estar	*to be*
O céu **está** azul.	*The sky **is** blue.*
(O céu) **está** nublado	***It is** cloudy.*

Não é/né? If you know some French, you will notice that this expression is used like the French **n'est-ce pas?**, meaning *isn't it?*

De interesse

In Portugal, ice-cream vendors walk along beaches in the summer with boxes full of ices. You can also buy snacks—potato chips, nuts—from beach vendors. On Brazilian beaches you can buy chilled fresh *coconut juice* (**água de coco**); wonderful to cool you down in that Brazilian heat.

Ill health

Precautions in the sun

11

VOCABULÁRIO

bom/boa/bons/boas	*good*
bronzeador	*tanning*
clara [f.]	*fair (skin or hair coloring)*
creme [m.]	*cream*
esta [f.]	*this, this one*
este [m.]	*this, this one*
fator [m.]	*factor*
óleo [m.]	*oil*
pele [f.]	*skin*
precisa (de)	*you need*
queimaduras [f., pl.]	*burns*
recomendo	*I recommend*
sol [m.]	*sun*
solar	*to sun (adjective)*
ter/tomar cuidado	*to take care*
usar	*to use*
vez [f.]	*time*
vezes [f., pl.]	*times*

Diálogo

WOMAN: Têm creme para queimaduras do sol?

PHARMACIST: Temos, sim, senhora. Este é muito bom. Precisa de usar duas vezes por dia.

WOMAN: Obrigada. Também têm óleo bronzeador?

PHARMACIST: Temos, mas a pele da senhora é muito clara—precisa de usar um bom creme solar. Recomendo o fator número quinze. Este é bom.

WOMAN: Obrigadinha. O sol está muito bom agora.

PHARMACIST: Claro que está, mas precisa de ter muito cuidado com o sol aqui em Portugal.

To say this you use **este** (m.) or **esta** (f.); to say these, **estes** (m., pl.) or **estas** (f., pl.). Decide which one is correct in each of the following sentences and then translate them into English. The first one is done to guide you.

1. _Esta_ camisa é cara.   _This shirt is expensive._

2. _____ céu está azul.   _____

3. _____ sapatos são bons.   _____

4. _____ senhor é bonito.   _____

5. _____ senhora é clara.   _____

6. _____ sapatos não são caros.   _____

Listen to a pharmacist recommending suncreams of various factors to different people and telling them how many times a day they must use them. Fill in the table below with your answers.

FACTOR NO.   TIMES PER DAY

1. _____   _____

2. _____   _____

Now imagine you are the pharmacist, and for each person on the recording who asks you for suncream, follow the instructions below for your recommendations. The presenter will guide you.

RECOMMENDED FACTOR	TIMES PER DAY
1. 15	3
2. 12	1

Língua

You will have noticed the words for *good* in the **vocabulário**. There are four forms.

	Singular		Plural	
Masculine	**bom** dia	*good morning*	**bons** sapatos	*good shoes*
Feminine	**boa** noite	*good evening/night*	**boas** pessoas	*good people*

This adjective tends to go in front of the noun it is describing, whereas most other adjectives go afterwards.

The verb *to need* in Portuguese is **precisar (de)**. When it is followed by a noun it requires the word **de** after it, otherwise it can be followed immediately by a verb in the infinitive, which often happens in Brazil. The **de** combines with the words for *the* (**o/a/os/as**) and *a/some* (**um/uma/uns/umas**).

Precisa do creme.	*You need the cream.*
Precisa (de) usar um creme.	*You need to use a cream.*

De interesse

The sun in Portugal and Brazil can be extremely hot in the summer months. Although Portuguese people do not really take a siesta, as their Spanish counterparts do, most shops close from 1–3 P.M., and sensible people sit inside where it is cooler. Brazilians love the *beach* (**a praia**). In Rio the coolest, most beautiful people parade themselves in Copacabana, Ipanema, and Leblon, but amazing beaches can be found all round Brazil's extensive coastline.

Time

The best time for doing things

VOCABULÁRIO	
à praia	to the beach
aconselhável	advisable
as nove (horas)	nine o'clock
as seis (horas)	six o'clock
até	until
com	with
da manhã	in the morning
da tarde	in the afternoon
depois (de)	after
deveria	I (you, he, she, it) should
entre	between
essa [f.]	that
ficar	to stay
ir	to go
meio-dia [m.]	midday
melhor	better
poderia	you (I, he, she, it) could
primeiro	first
tome	take
vinte	20
vinte e um/uma	21
vinte e dois/duas	22
vinte e três	23
vinte e quatro	24
vinte e cinco	25
vinte e seis	26
vinte e sete	27
vinte e oito	28
vinte e nove	29
trinta	30
quarenta	40
cinquenta	50
sessenta	60
setenta	70
oitenta	80
noventa	90
cem, cento	100

Diálogo

TOURIST: Qual é a melhor hora para ir à praia?

WOMAN: Bom, agora, entre as nove da manhã e o meio-dia, ou depois das seis da tarde.

TOURIST: E quanto tempo deveria ficar?

WOMAN: Pois, com essa pele clara, é aconselhável só ficar vinte e cinco minutos no primeiro dia.

TOURIST: E depois?

WOMAN: Depois, poderia ficar mais, até quarenta ou cinquenta minutos por dia, mas tome muito cuidado.

ATIVIDADE 12·1

Four people have asked how long they should stay on the beach. Match up the replies to the time indicated on the clocks.

1. Poderia ficar trinta e cinco minutos.

2. É aconselhável só ficar vinte minutos.

3. É melhor ficar quarenta minutos.

4. Poderia ficar cinquenta e cinco minutos.

a.

b.

c.

d.

ATIVIDADE 12·2

Now listen to some numbers on the recording, and circle those you hear.

55	96	31	78	24	49
62	34	29	83	97	57
43	71	38	66	45	92

The table below indicates how long you can safely stay on beaches around the world. Answer the questions on the recording by referring to the table.

BEACH	NUMBER OF MINUTES
Lisboa	48
Rio	22
California	34
Brighton	97
Alicante	55
Madeira	61

Língua

From the vocabulary list on page 34, you will be able to work out how numbers above 20 are put together. You simply insert the word for *and* (**e**) between the two digits. You will find this pattern occurring again when you move on to higher numbers.

If your last digit is a 1 or 2, you always have to choose between the masculine or feminine forms of those numbers, depending on the gender (m. or f.) of the following noun.

There are two words for 100: **cem** for a round one hundred, and **cento** for anything over a hundred; for example, 102 tickets = **cento e dois bilhetes**.

De interesse

Most Portuguese families sit under huge sunshades on the beach and take enormous picnics in coolers so that a day on the beach is enjoyable and sunstroke-free. Young Portuguese and Brazilian people love playing sports on the beach—**futebol** (*football*), **volei** (*volleyball*) and **surfe** (*surfing*).

People

Getting to know people

·13·

---

alemão	*German*
Como está?	*How are you?*
Estou bem.	*I'm well.*
Fala . . . ?	*Do you speak . . . ?*
fala bem	*you speak well*
falo	*I speak*
Francês	*French*
não falo	*I don't speak*
Português	*Portuguese*
um pouco (de)	*a little, a bit (of)*

Diálogo

ANNE GREEN: Boa tarde, Senhor Silva. Como está?

ANTÓNIO DA SILVA: Boa tarde, Anne. Estou bem, obrigado. E a Anne? Como está?

ANNE GREEN: Muito bem, obrigada.

ANTÓNIO DA SILVA: A Anne fala bem português.

ANNE GREEN: Obrigada. O senhor fala inglês?

ANTÓNIO DA SILVA: Falo um pouco. Falo francês também. A Anne fala francês?

ANNE GREEN: Não, não falo, mas falo um pouco de alemão.

ATIVIDADE
13·1

Check the appropriate boxes for each of the languages each person speaks.

	FRENCH	ENGLISH	PORTUGUESE	GERMAN
1. Falo inglês, alemão e um pouco de francês.	☐	☐	☐	☐
2. Não falo francês, mas falo português bem.	☐	☐	☐	☐
3. Falo um pouco de alemão.	☐	☐	☐	☐

ATIVIDADE
13·2

Listen to the people on the recording saying which languages they speak, and how well. Fill in their details in the table below. Put one check mark if they do speak the language, two check marks if they speak it well, and a cross if they don't speak it.

	FRENCH	ENGLISH	GERMAN	PORTUGUESE
1.	_____	_____	_____	_____
2.	_____	_____	_____	_____
3.	_____	_____	_____	_____
4.	_____	_____	_____	_____

ATIVIDADE 13·3

Now take part in a dialogue, using the prompts below to guide you. Speak in the pauses.

1. Hello, I'm well, thank you.

2. And how are you?

3. Thank you. Do you speak English?

4. I speak a bit of German and also some French.

Língua

The words for the different languages are identical to the masculine word for nationalities. Therefore, **francês** can mean not only the French language but also a Frenchman. Most of the feminine forms will be formed by adding an **–a** to the masculine word, although there are a few exceptions.

Masculine	Feminine	Masc. Pl.	Fem. Pl.
francês	francesa	franceses	francesas
inglês	inglesa	ingleses	inglesas
português	portuguesa	portugueses	portuguesas
alemão	alemã	alemães	alemãs

All these words are also adjectives, describing where things and people are from: **uma cidade inglesa** (*an English city*), **camisas alemãs** (*German shirts*). The adjectives come after the words they are describing.

De interesse

In Portugal, when people are on more friendly terms you will hear them refer to each other with **o** or **a** + the person's name. See the table below:

	Formal	More Informal
Masculine	o senhor	o Luís
Feminine	a senhora	a Anne

Brazilians tend to stick to using **você**.

Eating out
Making choices

Diálogo

CUSTOMER 1: Faz favor!

WAITER: Bom dia, senhores. O que vão tomar?

CUSTOMER 1: Bom, para mim é um chá com leite e uma fatia de bolo de amêndoa.

WAITER: E para a senhora?

CUSTOMER 2: O que tem de sanduíches?

WAITER: De sandes temos queijo, fiambre, ovo e atum.

CUSTOMER 2: Então quero uma de queijo, se faz favor.

WAITER: E para beber?

CUSTOMER 2: Para mim pode ser uma bica.

Fill in the spaces with the following words:

sanduíche   a   uma   fatia   bolo   pode   é   com

1. Para mim, _____ uma bica e uma _____ de _____ de amêndoa.

2. Para _____ senhora, é um chá _____ leite e uma _____ de ovo.

3. Para José _____ ser uma bica e _____ sandes de queijo.

Listen to the speakers ordering in a café and decide whether the statements below are true (**verdadeiro**) *or false* (**falso**).

	V	F
Speaker 1 wants a ham sandwich and an espresso coffee.	___	___
Speaker 2 wants some chocolate cake and an egg sandwich.	___	___
Speaker 3 would like a white coffee and two tuna sandwiches.	___	___

Now take part in a dialogue in a café. Follow the prompts below.

1. For me, a small black coffee and a slice of chocolate cake.

2. What have you got in sandwiches?

3. Well, I'm going to have an egg one, please.

Língua

The word **é** is from the verb *to be* (**ser**), and it means *is* (or *you are*). You came across it earlier, in Unit 9. It is frequently used when ordering food and drink, instead of saying *I'll have*. You can say *for me, it's a—* . . . *—***para mim, é um/uma** . . . .

De interesse

There are a variety of places to eat in Portugal and Brazil. There is the **café** (a word that means both *coffee* and *café*) and there is also the **pastelaria**. Although this means literally *the cake shop*, these places mostly have tables for you to sit down and gorge yourself on the wonderful **bolos** and **pastéis**! Brazilians enjoy a visit to a **lanchonete** (*snack bar*) and more often prefer savory snacks such as burgers or **pão de queijo** (*cheesy bread*).

Accommodations

Reserving a room

15

VOCABULÁRIO

incluído	*included*
pequeno almoço [m.]; [BP] o café da manhã	*breakfast*
casa de banho [f.]; [BP] o banheiro	*bathroom*
Para que dia?	*For which day?*
pousada [f.]	*historic hotel/inn*
Pretende ficar?	*(Do) You intend to stay?*
Quer . . . ?	*Do you want . . . ?*
reservar	*to reserve*
sem	*without*
janeiro	*January*
fevereiro	*February*
março	*March*
abril	*April*
maio	*May*
junho	*June*
julho	*July*
agosto	*August*
setembro	*September*
outubro	*October*
novembro	*November*
dezembro	*December*

Diálogo

RECEPTIONIST: Pousada dos Lóios, bom dia.

CUSTOMER: Bom dia. Queria reservar um quarto individual, se faz favor.

RECEPTIONIST: Para que dia?

CUSTOMER: Para o dia vinte e cinco de maio.

RECEPTIONIST: Quantas noites pretende ficar?

CUSTOMER: Quatro.

RECEPTIONIST: Quer com ou sem casa de banho?

CUSTOMER: Com, se faz favor.

ATIVIDADE 15·1

Match the captions to the pictures.

1. Um quarto simples com casa de banho e pequeno almoço. _____

2. Um quarto de casal com casa de banho para três noites. _____

3. Um quarto individual sem banheiro para uma noite. _____

4. Um quarto simples com casa de banho, sem pequeno almoço. _____

a.

b.

c.

d.

ATIVIDADE 15·2

*Listen to the customers on the recording reserving rooms in a **pousada** and mark in the columns below what is required by each one.*

	QUARTO		CASA DE BANHO		PEQUENO ALMOÇO	
	individual	casal	com	sem	incluído	não incluído
1.	_____	_____	_____	_____	_____	_____
2.	_____	_____	_____	_____	_____	_____

ATIVIDADE 15·3

Now take part in a dialogue with a hotel receptionist. Follow the prompts below.

1. Good afternoon. I would like to reserve a double room.

2. For the 27th of January.

3. Two.

4. With, please.

Língua

The months are now all written in Portuguese with a small first letter. This comes about as a result of the recent Spelling Agreement, which came into force in 2007. You will still find examples of the months with a capital first letter, though, as it will take up to ten years to modify all written material.

De interesse

Pousadas are the Portuguese equivalent of the Spanish *paradors*. They are luxury inns and hotels, usually located in beautiful old buildings, such as castles, monasteries and manor houses. Other forms of accommodation in Portugal include **pensão** (*bed and breakfast*), the **residência/residencial** (*guest house*), and the **albergaria/estalagem** (*inn*). In Brazil, you might typically stay in a hotel (pronounced 'otel') of varying quality, or even an **albergue de juventude** (*youth hostel*). The term **pousada** in Brazil just means a guesthouse.

16

Travel

A train journey

VOCABULÁRIO	
(o) seu troco	*your change*
comboio [m.]; [BP] o trem	*train*
Daqui a vinte minutos.	*In twenty minutes.*
de primeira classe	*first class*
de segunda classe	*second class*
linha [f.]	*platform*
parte	*it departs*
partida [f.]	*departure*
Qual é a linha?	*Which platform is it?*
Qual é . . . ?	*Which is . . . ?*
Quanto tempo falta para . . . ?	*How much time is there before . . . ?*
uma nota	*a note (monetary)*
duzentos	200
trezentos	300
quatrocentos	400
quinhentos	500
seiscentos	600
setecentos	700
oitocentos	800
novecentos	900
mil	1,000

🄍 Diálogo

TRAVELER: Faz favor, queria um bilhete de ida e volta para o Porto.

TICKET CLERK: De primeira ou segunda classe?

TRAVELER: De segunda. Qual é a linha?

TICKET CLERK: O comboio parte da linha número seis.

TRAVELER: Quanto tempo falta para a partida?

TICKET CLERK: O comboio parte daqui a vinte minutos.

*You have gone on a shopping spree in Brazil with 500 **Reais** (Brazilian reals). Read the **Língua** section on how to form numbers in the hundreds, then check the price tags on these items and match them to the correct amounts written below.*

Quanto custa? *How much does it cost?*

1. R 345
2. R 492
3.  R 124
4. R 268
5.  R 170

a. Cento e vinte e quatro reais _____

b. Trezentos e quarenta e cinco reais _____

c. Cento e setenta reais _____

d. Quatrocentos e noventa e dois reais _____

e. Duzentos e sessenta e oito reais _____

ATIVIDADE
16·2

Listen to someone asking for train tickets and answer the following questions in English.

1. First or second class?

2. The train leaves from which platform?

3. The train is due to leave in how many minutes?

ATIVIDADE
16·3

Now take part in a dialogue yourself, based on the one on the previous page. Use the prompts below to guide you. You start.

1. I'd like a return ticket to Braga, please.

2. First class.

3. Which platform is it?

Língua

When you are dealing with higher numbers, the word **e** (*and*) appears between the hundred and ten and unit; for example, 156—**cento *e* cinquenta *e* seis**.

After thousands, there is usually just a pause; for example, 1,278-**mil, duzentos e setenta e oito**.

However, the word **e** appears after the thousand if the number following is anything from 1 to 100; for example, 1,089—**mil *e* oitenta e nove**, or when the number following ends in two zeros (200–900); for example, 6,300—**seis mil *e* trezentos**.

The numbers 200–900 also have a feminine form, used for feminine words such as **milhas** (*miles*); for example, **trezentas milhas** (*300 miles*).

De interesse

If you need to change money in Portugal or Brazil, the following vocabulary might be useful:

casa de câmbio	*bureau de change*	**compra**	*buying*
câmbio	*currency exchange*	**venda**	*selling*
cotação/taxa de câmbio	*rate of exchange*	**moeda**	*coin/currency*
taxa de comisão	*commission fee*	**nota**	*note*

Portugal	**o euro/o cêntimo**	*euro/cents*
Brazil	**o real/o centavo**	*real/cents*
USA	**o dólar**	*dollar*
United Kingdom	**a libra (esterlina)**	*pounds (sterling)*

Directions

Finding out where the bank is

VOCABULÁRIO	
ao lado de	*next to*
atravessa	*(you) cross*
detrás de	*behind*
museu [m.]	*museum*
Onde fica . . .?; [BP] *and also*	*Where is . . .?*
[EP] **Onde é . . .?**	
ora bem	*well now*
para trás	*back/round*
passa	*(you) pass*
pela [f.]	*through, by the*
por	*through, by, along*
volta	*(you) turn/return*

Diálogo

VISITOR: Faz favor. Onde fica o banco?

MAN: Ora bem. A senhora vira aqui à esquerda, passa pela Praça São Vicente, e o banco fica ao lado do cinema.

VISITOR: Muito obrigada.

MAN: De nada.

VISITOR: Desculpe, onde fica a Praça São Vicente?

PASSERBY: A Praça São Vicente? Pois, a senhora volta para trás, atravessa a avenida, e a praça fica detrás do museu.

Which bank are you looking for? Fill in the appropriate word(s) to indicate where each bank is located.

1.

a. O Banco Forte fica _____ cinema.

2.

b. O Banco Rico fica _____ Camões.

3.

c. O Banco d'Ouro fica _____ museu.

4.

d. O Banco Soares fica _____ turismo.

The Banco Gordo is in the Praça Municipal, next to the butcher. Listen to two people asking where the bank is and decide which one of them has been given the true location.

VERDADEIRO   FALSO

1. _____   _____

2. _____   _____

Take part in a dialogue as you try to find out where the bank is. You start.

1. Where is the bank?

2. Excuse me, can you repeat that more slowly, please?

3. Is it far?

4. Thank you very much.

Língua

In the dialogue we had another example of two words combining, or contracting: **pela praça** (*through the square*). This is a combination of the word **por** (*by/through*), plus **a** (*the*).

	Singular	Plural
por	+ o → pelo	+ os → pelos
	+ a → pela	+ as → pelas
	pelos parques	*through the parks*
	pelas avenidas	*through/along the avenues*

De interesse

Museums and other cultural institutions in Portugal usually close on Mondays. Banks generally open from 8:30 until 3:30, or from about 9–2 or 3 P.M. in Brazil. Most offer a wide range of services, including **câmbio** (*exchange*), and in most large towns you will find automatic cash dispensers (**Multibanco**, or **caixa automático** in Brazil) for use with credit cards.

Town amenities

At the bank

VOCABULÁRIO

(a) sua morada	*your address*
à caixa [f.]	*at, to the cash desk*
assinar	*to sign*
cada	*each (one)*
chapa [f.]	*small disc (see De interesse)*
em total	*in all*
leva	*(you) take*
libras esterlinas [f., pl.]	*pounds sterling*
morada [f.]; [BP] *and also* [EP] o endereço	*address*
o seu [m.], a sua [f.]	*your*
para receber	*(in order) to receive*
passaporte [m.]	*passport*
portanto	*so, in that case*
Quantos...?	*How many...?*
trocar	*to change*

Diálogo

VISITOR: Queria trocar estes 'travellers cheques,' se faz favor.

BANK CLERK: Com certeza. Quantos tem?

VISITOR: Tenho dez cheques, de cinquenta libras cada.

BANK CLERK: Portanto, são quinhentas libras esterlinas em total. Tem o seu passaporte?

VISITOR: Aqui está.

BANK CLERK: Qual é a sua morada aqui em Portugal?

VISITOR: É o Hotel Miraflores, Avenida de São João, número vinte e quatro, Braga.

BANK CLERK: Faz o favor de assinar os cheques. A senhora leva esta chapa à caixa para receber o dinheiro.

Match the captions to the correct pictures by drawing a line between them.

1. trezentos e cinquenta dólares

a.

2. um passaporte

b.

3. a morada em Portugal

c.

4. assinar os cheques

d.

5. esta chapa

e.

6. receber o dinheiro

f.

Listen to someone at the bank and fill in the information from the transaction in the table below.

QUANTOS CHEQUES?	DINHEIRO EM TOTAL	HOTEL NAME	HOTEL ADDRESS
_____	_____	_____	_____

ATIVIDADE
18·3

Take part in a dialogue in a bank using the prompts below. You start.

1. I'd like to change these travelers checks.

2. Five, twenty pounds each one.

3. Here it is.

4. Hotel Palácio, Rua Principal, number 36, Nazaré

Língua

The form for *your* depends on the gender (m. or f.) and number (singular or plural) of the word that follows, and not on the person doing the possessing. Therefore, you must know whether the possessed item is masculine or feminine, singular or plural.

noun	your		
o dinheiro	(o) seu	(o) seu dinheiro	*your money*
a morada	(a) sua	(a) sua morada	*your address*
os bolos	(os) seus	(os) seus bolos	*your cakes*
as camisas	(as) suas	(as) as suas camisas	*your shirts*

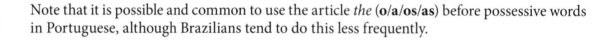

Note that it is possible and common to use the article *the* (**o/a/os/as**) before possessive words in Portuguese, although Brazilians tend to do this less frequently.

De interesse

Not all banks in Portugal hand out **chapas** these days, but if you are handed a disc with a number on it, you need to go and wait where the sign says **caixa** (*cashier*) and listen for the number to be called so that you don't miss your turn to get your money.

54   PRACTICE MAKES PERFECT   Beginning Portuguese

Downtown

Buying clothes at the shopping center

19

VOCABULÁRIO

alguma coisa [f.]	*something*
amarelo	*yellow*
aquela [f.]	*that (one)*
blusa [f.]	*blouse*
centro comercial [m.]	*shopping center/mall*
cor [f.]	*color*
cor-de-rosa	*pink*
custam	*they cost*
encontrar	*to find*
experimentar	*to try (on)*
levo	*I'll take*
padrão [m.]	*style*
tamanho [m.]	*size*
uma loja de roupas	*a clothes shop*
vários/as [pl.]	*various, several*
verde	*green*

Diálogo

WOMAN: Desculpe. Onde é que posso encontrar uma loja de roupas?

MAN: Pois, há várias aqui no centro comercial.

WOMAN: Bom dia. Quero comprar uma blusa.

ASSISTANT: Temos vários padrões e cores. Qual é o seu tamanho?

WOMAN: É o quarenta e dois. Tem alguma coisa em azul?

ASSISTANT: Temos esta em azul, esta em verde ou em amarelo, e temos aquela em cor-de-rosa.

WOMAN: Posso experimentar estas duas?

ASSISTANT: Claro que pode.

WOMAN: Quanto custa esta?

ASSISTANT: Duzentos.

WOMAN: E aquela?

ASSISTANT: Cento e noventa.

WOMAN: Então levo esta. Obrigada.

ATIVIDADE
19·1

Match the Portuguese with the English sentences about buying a blouse.

1. Quero esta blusa verde.

2. Levo esta blusa, tamanho quarenta e dois.

3. Posso experimentar aquela blusa azul?

4. Quanto custa esta em amarelo?

5. Quero aquela no tamanho 42.

a. I'll take this blouse, size 42.

b. How much does this one cost in yellow?

c. I want this green blouse.

d. I want that one in size 42.

e. Can I try on that blue blouse?

ATIVIDADE
19·2

Listen to someone buying a blouse in a shop and write the details in the table below.

	BLUE	PINK	GREEN	YELLOW
What size?	_____	_____	_____	_____
Colors shown?	_____	_____	_____	_____
Color chosen?	_____	_____	_____	_____

ATIVIDADE
19·3

Now take part in a dialogue yourself, following the prompts below.

1. Say good morning and that you'd like to buy a blouse.

2. Answer the question. [size 38] Ask if there's anything in green.

3. Ask if you can try on that one.

Feminine		Masculine	Feminine
...ta	*these*	**estes**	**estas**
...quela	*those*	**aqueles**	**aquelas**
estas camisas		*these shirts*	
aqueles sapatos		*those shoes*	

...easingly popular in larger Portuguese towns. The most ...l Amoreiras in Lisbon, which was a controversial departure ...30s. There is now an even bigger one called the Centro ... their *shopping malls* as **o shopping**.

Personal choices

When do you usually go shopping?

VOCABULÁRIO	
ando muito ocupado/a	*I'm very busy*
aos fins de semana	*at the weekends(s)*
às vezes	*sometimes*
de vez em quando	*sometimes*
em geral	*generally*
faço	*I do, make*
fazer as compras	*to do the shopping*
fazes as compras	*you (fam.) do the shopping*
feira [f.]	*monthly market*
geralmente	*generally*
gostas de ir	*you like to go*
mercado [m.]	*market*
muitas vezes	*often*
nas terças	*on Tuesdays*
nem sempre	*not always*
poucas vezes	*little (seldom)*
quase nunca	*hardly ever*
sempre	*always*
supermercado [m.]	*supermarket*
tu	*you (fam.)*
uma pechincha	*a bargain*
Vais . . .	*(Do) You go . . .*
vou	*I go*

🔘 Diálogo

JOÃO: Olá, Maria, boa tarde. Então, sempre fazes as compras nas terças?

MARIA: Nem sempre, João. Geralmente vou ao supermercado nas segundas, mas esta semana ando muito ocupada.

JOÃO: Pessoalmente, prefiro fazer as compras aos fins de semana, mas de vez em quando vou nas quartas. Vais muitas vezes ao mercado?

MARIA: Em geral faço as compras no mercado três vezes por semana. Às vezes vou à feira—sempre há uma pechincha. E tu, João quando é que gostas de ir à feira?

JOÃO: À feira, pois, poucas vezes, quase nunca. Gosto mais do centro comercial.

ATIVIDADE 20·1

Match up the Portuguese and English phrases.

1. Às vezes vou ao supermercado.

2. Nunca vou à feira.

3. Vou ao mercado, em geral.

4. Vou muitas vezes à feira.

5. Sempre faço as compras no mercado.

a. Generally I go to the market.

b. Sometimes I go to the supermarket.

c. I often go to the monthly market.

d. I never go to the monthly market.

e. I always shop at the market.

ATIVIDADE 20·2

Listen to Paula and José talking about their shopping habits and write down in the table how often they go to the places below.

	MARKET	SUPERMARKET	MONTHLY MARKET
José	_____	_____	_____
Paula	_____	_____	_____

ATIVIDADE 20·3

Someone will now ask you when you usually do the shopping. Use the prompts below to guide you.

1. Not always, sometimes I do the shopping in the supermarket.

2. I hardly ever go to the monthly market.

3. Generally, I shop there on Thursdays, but this week I'm very busy.

Língua

Up to now, you have learned verb forms and forms of address in polite terms, using either **o senhor/a senhora**, or **o/a** + the person's name. If you know someone well, or if you are talking to a member of your family or a young person, you can be less formal, and call them **tu** (*you*), as you will see in the dialogue. The verb forms are also different—the **tu** form has an **–s** ending.

Verb		Polite Form	Familiar Form	
gostar	*to like*	**gosta**	**gostas**	*you like*
ir	*to go*	**vai**	**vais**	*you go*
fazer	*to make/do*	**faz**	**fazes**	*you make/do*

In Brazil, this **tu** form of the verb is only found in a few areas; use **você** as your main form of address there.

De interesse

The **feiras** are very popular in Portugal. They are generally monthly markets, selling everything from pots and baskets to clothes and farming utensils, as well as the usual food produce. Often moving from one village to another throughout the month, the Algarve **feiras** are often run by gypsies and are colorful shopping grounds.

Vacations

Where and when do you spend your holidays?

·21·

VOCABULÁRIO

(n)a primavera	*(in) spring*
(n)o inverno	*(in) winter*
(n)o outono	*(in) autumn*
(n)o verão	*(in) summer*
Alemanha [f.]	*Germany*
calmo	*quiet, calm*
campo [m.]	*countryside*
costa [f.]	*coast*
França [f.]	*France*
fresco	*cool, fresh*
Grécia [f.]	*Greece*
ir de férias	*to go on holiday*
Japão [m.]	*Japan*
lindo	*pretty*
Onde costumas . . . ?	*Where do you (fam.) usually . . . ?*
paisagem [f.]	*scenery*
passear	*to visit, stroll, wander*
passo	*I spend*
Portugal	*Portugal*
Suíça [f.]	*Switzerland*
tiro	*I take*
viajar	*to travel*
Vou para . . .	*I go to . . .*

Diálogo

JOANA: Olá, Pedro! Então, vais de férias outra vez?

PEDRO: Sempre tiro as férias no inverno.

JOANA: Onde costumas passar as férias?

PEDRO: Em geral, passo as férias de inverno na Suíça porque a paisagem é muito linda.

JOANA: Prefiro viajar no outono quando o campo está mais calmo. Vou muitas vezes para a Grécia ou, de vez em quando, para a França.

PEDRO: E no verão, Joana, não gostas de viajar?

JOANA: Nunca tiro férias no verão—gosto mais de passear na costa, onde está mais fresco. E tu, Pedro?

PEDRO: Gosto de visitar o Japão, a Alemanha, ou Portugal, claro!

ATIVIDADE 21·1

For each statement, write down in English when and where the people prefer to go on holiday. The first one is an example for you.

1. Gosto de visitar a Grécia no inverno.

2. Prefiro viajar no Japão no verão.

3. Sempre passo as férias de primavera na Alemanha.

4. Gosto de passear em Portugal no inverno.

5. Tiro as férias de outono na Suíça.

SEASON	COUNTRY
a. *winter*	*Greece*
b. _____	_____
c. _____	_____
d. _____	_____
e. _____	_____

ATIVIDADE
21·2

Listen to someone being interviewed about their holidays, and fill in the table below with their destinations.

SPRING	SUMMER	AUTUMN	WINTER

ATIVIDADE
21·3

Now it's your turn to talk about holidays. Follow the prompts below and take part in the dialogue.

1. I spend the spring holidays in France because the scenery is very pretty.

2. I never go on holiday in the summer.

3. In the autumn I like to visit Portugal, when the coast is quieter.

Língua

Countries' names are either masculine or feminine, and are mostly used with the appropriate **o/a** before them. One of the exceptions is **Portugal** itself, which does not use **o** or **a**. Additional countries you may want to make a note of include:

os Estados Unidos	*United States*	**a Inglaterra**	*England*
a Dinamarca	*Denmark*	**o México**	*Mexico*
o Brasil	*Brazil*	**a Escócia**	*Scotland*
a Espanha	*Spain*	**a Irlanda**	*Ireland*

De interesse

Most Portuguese people take their holidays in the summer. The Algarve and the northern coastline (Costa da Prata) are very popular with Portuguese from the north. They also like to visit family in the rural areas, often uprooting themselves to the countryside for a few hot weeks.

The weather

Talking about bad weather

VOCABULÁRIO

ano [m.]	*year*
castanhas [f., pl.]	*chestnuts*
chuva [f.]	*rain*
como	*as/like*
estranho	*strange*
faz frio	*it's cold*
hoje em dia	*nowadays*
neve [f.]	*snow*
normal	*normal*
nublado	*cloudy*
o mau tempo	*the bad weather*
péssimo	*terrible*
pois(é); [BP] é mesmo/é verdade	*that's right*
que bom	*(how) good/lovely*
quente	*hot*
razoável	*reasonable*
tem razão	*you're right*
um pacote	*a packet*

Diálogo

CHESTNUT VENDOR: Castanhas quentes! Castanhas quentes!

WOMAN: Que bom! Um pacote, se faz favor. Que mau tempo temos.

CHESTNUT VENDOR: Tem razão. Hoje está um dia péssimo.
Faz muito frio e o céu está nublado.

WOMAN: Mas este tempo é normal aqui no inverno?

CHESTNUT VENDOR: Não muito, não. Em geral temos tempo
razoável, mas este ano há mais chuva e vento.

WOMAN: Como na Inglaterra também. Hoje em dia o tempo é
estranho.

CHESTNUT VENDOR: Pois é.

ATIVIDADE

22·1

Match up the Portuguese and English weather expressions.

1. Faz frio.

2. O céu está nublado.

3. Tem neve.

4. Há chuva.

5. Há muito vento.

a. It's snowing.

b. It's cold.

c. It's raining.

d. The sky is cloudy.

e. It's very windy.

ATIVIDADE

22·2

Listen to these descriptions of the weather in two Portuguese cities, and decide which picture relates to each city.

1.  3°C _____

2. _____

ATIVIDADE

22·3

Now take part in a dialogue about bad weather. Follow the prompts below.

1. Good, I'll have two packets, please.

2. You're right. It's cold and cloudy.

3. Sometimes, but this year there is more wind.

4. Today is a terrible day for the beach.

Língua

Pois é, like the word **pois** on its own, is extremely common in Portuguese conversations, as a stopgap. It can mean: *that's right, that's it, well, yes,* or even just *mmm!* Brazilians use similar pause devices, such as **ah é?** (*really?*) and **tá** (for **está**—*OK*).

De interesse

In some Portuguese regions, such as the flat expanse of land in the centre of the country, the Alentejo, or the hilly Trás-os-Montes in the north, the temperature can drop below freezing. In the Algarve the weather is temperamental in the winter. Some people have enjoyed Christmas on the beach, while for other visitors umbrellas and raincoats have been the order of the day.

In Brazil, too, there are huge differences—not surprising given the size of the place. The south has the most extremes of temperature, with very occasional snow in some parts.

Ill health

Getting a cold

VOCABULÁRIO	
algum [m.]	*some*
aspirina [f.]	*aspirin*
boa ideia [f.]	*good idea*
cama [f.]	*bed*
cansado	*tired*
clima [m.]	*weather, climate*
coitado	*poor thing*
descansar	*to rest*
estar a tomar; [BP] estar tomando	*to be taking*
estar constipado/a;	*to have a cold*
[BP] estar resfriado	
mudança [f.]	*change*
Não seria melhor . . . ?	*Wouldn't it be better . . . ?*
por causa de	*because of/on account of*
provavelmente	*probably*
remédio [m.]	*medicine, tablet*
Saúde!	*Bless you! (also Cheers!)*
uma dor de cabeça	*a headache*
uma dor de garganta	*a sore throat*
xarope [m.]	*cough medicine*

Diálogo

WOMAN: Aachoo!

MAN: Saúde!

WOMAN: Obrigada! Estou um pouco constipada. Acho que é por
causa da mudança do clima.

MAN: Provavelmente. Coitada! Estás a tomar algum remédio?

WOMAN: Sim, estou a tomar aspirina porque também tenho uma
dor de cabeça.

MAN: Não seria melhor ir descansar um pouco?

WOMAN: Boa ideia! Também tenho uma dor de garganta.
Vou tomar um xarope e vou para a cama. Estou muito cansada.

Complete the speech bubbles, then match each one to a suggested remedy.

Não seria melhor ...

Tenho uma dor de ....

1.

   a. tomar um xarope?

Tenho uma dor de ....

2.

   b. ir para a cama?

Aachoo! Estou ....

3.

   c. tomar uma aspirina?

_____

Listen to the following dialogue between two people who are suffering from colds.
Which speaker (male or female) has the sore throat?

_____

_____

Now take part in a dialogue about cold symptoms, following the prompts below.
Start with a sneeze, then speak in the pauses.

1. Thanks, I've got a cold.

2. I'm taking aspirin because I have a headache.

3. Good idea. I also have a sore throat and I'm very tired.

Língua

If you want to say you are doing something currently, or if you want to ask someone about their current actions, Portuguese uses the construction **estar** + **a** + action verb in the infinitive, which equates to the English *-ing* form.

Está a tomar . . . ?	*Are you taking . . . ?*
Sim, **estou a tomar . . .**	*Yes, I'm taking . . .*
Estamos a falar.	*We are talking.*
Tu **estás a passear.**	*You are strolling.*

In Brazil, the construction is: **estar** + verb with these endings:

-ar verbs	**-ando**
-er verbs	**-endo**
-ir verbs	**-indo**
Estou falando.	*I am speaking.*

De interesse

When you go to a pharmacy in Portugal you will find most of the medication you are used to at home. In any case, the pharmacists are very helpful and will guide you toward the nearest equivalent medicine they have. Brazilian pharmacists are also experienced and their supplies well stocked in larger cities. Many medicines in both countries go under generic names, so make sure you know the proper name of anything you may need while there.

Time

Opening and closing times

VOCABULÁRIO

A que horas . . . ?	*At what time . . . ?*
à uma	*at one o'clock*
aberto	*open*
abre	*(it) opens*
almoço [m.]	*lunch*
às oito e meia	*at 8:30*
às seis menos dez	*at ten to six (lit. six minus ten)*
às três e um quarto	*at 3:15*
até às oito e vinte	*until 8:20*
das sete menos um quarto	*from a quarter to seven*
depois	*then, after*
farmácia [f.] de urgência	*emergency/on-service pharmacy*
fecha	*(it) closes*
fechado	*closed*
mesmo ali	*right there*
reabre	*(it) opens again*
Sabe . . . ?	*Do you know . . . ?*

🔘 Diálogo

TOURIST: Desculpe, sabe a que horas abre a farmácia?

WOMAN: Há uma farmácia aqui que abre às oito e meia da manhã.

TOURIST: E a que horas fecha?

WOMAN: Fecha à uma para o almoço. Depois, reabre às três e um quarto, e fecha às seis menos dez.

TOURIST: Preciso duma farmácia agora.

WOMAN: Há uma farmácia de urgência mesmo ali, que abre das sete menos um quarto até às oito e vinte.

TOURIST: Obrigado.

Match up the captions with the opening and closing times of the shops below.

1. Abre às dez menos um quarto da manhã. _____

2. Abre às oito e um quarto da manhã. _____

3. Fecha às nove e meia. _____

4. Fecha às cinco menos vinte e cinco. _____

5. Abre às oito menos vinte. _____

a. Banco Real 8:15 A.M.–4:15 P.M.

d. Livraria Cultural 9:45 A.M.–6:45 P.M.

b. Café Bom 8:00 A.M.–4:35 P.M.

e. Pastelaria Sabor 7:40 A.M.–10:00 P.M.

c. Loja de Roupas Finas 10:30 A.M.–9:30 P.M.

Listen to two people asking about opening and closing times of different places, and fill in the missing information in the table below.

PLACE	OPENS	CLOSES	LUNCH HOUR
1. <u>Museum</u>	_____	_____	_____
2. _____	<u>7:00 A.M.</u>	_____	_____

Now imagine someone asks you about the opening times of the local bank. Use the signs below to guide you and take part in a dialogue on the recording.

1   2   3

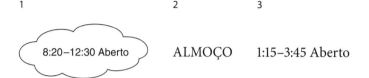

8:20–12:30 Aberto   ALMOÇO   1:15–3:45 Aberto

Língua

Time

à uma (hora)	*at 1:00*
às duas (horas)	*at 2:00*
às doze horas	*at 12:00*
ao meio-dia	*at midday*
à meia-noite	*at midnight*
às três (horas) e dez (minutos)	*at 3:10*
às quatro (horas) e quinze (minutos) **às quatro e um quarto**	*at 4:15*
às cinco (horas) e trinta (minutos) **às cinco e meia**	*at 5:30*
às seis (horas) e quarenta (minutos) **às sete menos vinte** **às vinte para as sete**	*at 6:40*
às sete (horas) e quarenta e cinco (minutos) **às oito menos um quarto** **a um quarto para as oito**	*at 7:45*

On timetables, the 24-hour clock is used, therefore:

vinte e uma (horas) e trinta e dois (minutos)   *21:32*

De interesse

Most shops in Portugal close from 1:00 to 3:00 P.M., and then open until 7:00 or 8:00 in the evening. In some shopping centers they stay open until 10:00 or 11:00 P.M. Restaurants seem to stay open until everyone has finished enjoying themselves! In Brazil, many shops open from 9–6:00 during the week, and 9–1:00 on Saturdays.

People

Talking about families

VOCABULÁRIO	
a minha mulher	*my wife*
ainda	*still*
apresentar	*to introduce*
casado/a	*married*
família [f.]	*family*
filha [f.]	*daughter*
filho [m.]	*son*
filhos [m., pl.]	*children, sons*
irmã [f.]	*sister*
irmão [m.]	*brother*
irmãos [m., pl.]	*brothers, brothers and sisters*
mãe [f.]	*mother*
marido [m.]	*husband*
mulher [f.]	*wife*
o marido dela	*her husband*
o meu marido	*my husband*
pai [m.]	*father*
pais [m., pl.]	*parents*
simpático/a	*nice, kind*
solteiro/a	*single*
Suécia [f.]	*Sweden*
sueco	*Swedish*
Tem saudades da família?	*Do you miss your family?*
vive	*he/she lives*
vivem	*they live*

Diálogo

ANTÓNIO DA SILVA: Olá, Anne. Queria apresentar a minha mulher, Maria da Graça.

ANNE GREEN: Muito prazer.

MARIA DA GRAÇA DA SILVA: Igualmente. A Anne é casada?

ANNE GREEN: Não, não sou. Ainda sou solteira.

ANTÓNIO DA SILVA: Mas tem família?

ANNE GREEN: Claro. Na minha família há o meu pai, a minha mãe eu e . . .

ANTÓNIO DA SILVA: Não tem irmãos?

ANNE GREEN: Sim, tenho. Tenho um irmão que vive nos Estados Unidos. É casado e tem três filhos—um filho e duas filhas. Também uma irmã. O marido dela é sueco. Vivem na Suécia.

ANTÓNIO DA SILVA: Tem saudades da família?

ANNE GREEN: Tenho, mas os portugueses são muito simpáticos.

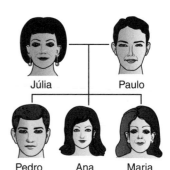

ATIVIDADE 25·1

Complete the sentences about this Portuguese family. Choose from the words listed.

os filhos   a irmã   o marido   a filha   casados   a mãe   o irmão
o filho   a mulher   o pai

1. A Júlia é _____ do Paulo.

2. O Paulo e a Júlia são _____.

3. O Paulo é _____ da Júlia.

4. A Júlia é _____ do Pedro, da Ana e da Maria.

5. O Paulo é _____ do Pedro, da Ana e da Maria.

6. O Pedro é _____ da Júlia.

7. A Ana é _____ do Paulo.

8. A Maria, o Pedro e a Ana são _____ da Júlia e do Paulo.

9. A Maria é _____ do Pedro.

10. O Pedro é _____ da Ana.

ATIVIDADE 25·2

Listen to two people describing their closest family and fill in their details in the table below. Write down how many children, brothers, and/or sisters they have.

	MARRIED	CHILDREN	BROTHERS	SISTERS
1.	_____	_____	_____	_____
2.	_____	_____	_____	_____

*Using the **Língua** notes below, give the Portuguese translation for the following sentences.*

1. He speaks English.

2. Do you (polite, masculine) live in Sweden?

3. They (feminine) are called Mary and Jean.

4. His brother lives in France.

5. Her husband is called José.

Língua

In this unit you are introduced to a verb in the plural, ie., describing the actions of more than one person. In most cases the pattern from singular to plural form in the present tense is like this:

Verb		he/she/it/you (polite)	they/you (pl.)
falar	*to speak*	**fala**	**falam**
chamar-se	*to be called*	**chama-se**	**chamam-se**
viver	*to live*	**vive**	**vivem**
abrir	*to open*	**abre**	**abrem**

The subjects of the verbs (those doing the action) can be expressed by means of the following pronouns:

I	*you* (fam.)	*he/it*	*she/it*	*you* (polite)	*we*	*you* (pl.)	*they* (m./f.)
eu	**tu**	**ele**	**ela**	**o/a senhor/a** **você**	**nós**	**os/as senhores/as** **vocês**	**eles/elas**

His/her can be conveyed by saying *the . . . of he/she*:

o marido **dela**	*her husband* (lit. *the husband of she*)
a mulher **dele**	*his wife* (lit. *the wife of he*)
O marido **dela** é sueco.	*Her husband is Swedish.*

De interesse

Portuguese and Brazilian families have traditionally been quite large, although these days not as large as they used to be.

Eating out

Ordering a meal for two

·26·

VOCABULÁRIO	
arroz doce [m.]	rice pudding (cold)
bacalhau à Brás [m.]	cod with eggs and potatoes
baunilha [f.]	vanilla
branco	white
caldo verde [m.]	shredded kale soup
carne de porco à alentejana [f.]	pork and clams Alentejo-style
e depois?	and then?
frango piri-piri [m.]	chicken piri-piri (spicy)
garrafa [f.]	bottle
leitão assado [m.]	roast sucking pig
lista [f.]; [BP] o cardápio; [EP] a ementa	menu
mousse de chocolate [f.]	chocolate mousse
papos de anjo [m., pl.]	egg-based sweet dessert
para começar	to start (with)
pudim [m.]	crème caramel
salada de frutas [f.]	fruit salad
sardinhas assadas [f., pl.]	grilled sardines
sobremesas [f., pl.]	desserts
sopa [f.] de agriões	watercress soup
sopa de legumes	vegetable soup
tinto	red wine
Vão querer . . . ?	Are you (pl.) going to want . . . ?
vinho [m.] da casa	house wine

Diálogo

CUSTOMER: A lista, se faz favor.

WAITER: Com certeza.

WAITER: Diga, se faz favor.

CUSTOMER: Para começar, é uma sopa de agriões e um caldo verde.

WAITER: Muito bem, e depois?

CUSTOMER: Para mim, pode ser a carne de porco à alentejana e, para o meu marido, um bacalhau à Brás.

WAITER: Vão querer sobremesas?

CUSTOMER: O que tem?

WAITER: Hoje há mousse de chocolate, arroz doce, pudim, salada de frutas e papos de anjo.

CUSTOMER: Então pode ser um pudim e uma mousse.

WAITER: E para beber?

CUSTOMER: Uma garrafa do vinho da casa.

WAITER: Tinto ou branco?

CUSTOMER: Tinto. Obrigada.

ATIVIDADE 26·1

Match the captions to the pictures.

1. uma salada de frutas

2. duas sopas

3. a lista/ementa

4. uma garrafa de vinho branco

5. duas garrafas de vinho tinto

a.

b.

EMENTA
Entradas ....
Peixa ....
Carne ....
Legumes ....
Sobremesas ....

c.

d.

e.

ATIVIDADE 26·2

Look at the menu for the Restaurante Imperial and listen to Mr. and Mrs. Gomes ordering a meal. Place a check mark next to the food and drink they order.

RESTAURANTE IMPERIAL

Hoje há

Sopa de legumes
Sopa de agriões
Caldo Verde

Mousse de chocolate
Bolo de amêndoa
Gelados — morango
— baunilha
— chocolate

Bacalhau à Brás
Carne de porco à alentejana
Frango piri-piri
Sardinhas assadas
Leitão assado

Vinho de casa — tinto
— branco

ATIVIDADE 26·3

Now see if you can order a meal for yourself and your brother. Use the prompts below to guide you and, if necessary, refer to the menu on the previous page. You start.

1. The menu, please.

2. To start with, one kale soup and one vegetable soup.

3. For me, the grilled sardines and, for my brother, the cod.

4. What is there?

5. Two fruit salads.

6. A bottle of house wine.

7. Red, thanks.

Língua

Vão is another example of a verb in the plural, this time from the irregular verb **ir** (*to go*). Here is the present tense in full:

eu	vou	*I go*	nós	vamos	*we go*
tu	vais	*you go*	os srs/as sras/vocês	vão	*you (pl.) go*
ele/ela	vai	*he/she/it goes*	eles/elas	vão	*they go*
o sr/a sra	vai	*you go (polite)*			
você	vai	*you go*			

De interesse

Portuguese cuisine is well-known for its heartiness and delicious combinations of **azeite de oliva** (*olive oil*), **alho** (*garlic*) and **temperos** (*spices*) such as piri-piri, brought back from far-off places by the navigators of old. It is also rather salty. **Carne de porco** (*pork*) is always a good choice, as is **peixe** (*fish*). The Portuguese eat a huge range of fish, the most famous being the typical *salted cod*, **o bacalhau**.

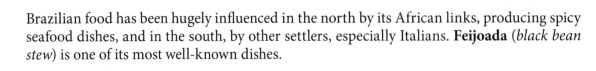

Brazilian food has been hugely influenced in the north by its African links, producing spicy seafood dishes, and in the south, by other settlers, especially Italians. **Feijoada** (*black bean stew*) is one of its most well-known dishes.

Accommodations

Checking into a campsite reservation

VOCABULÁRIO	
(Vocês) têm . . . ?	*Do you (pl.) have . . . ?*
ao fundo de	*at the far end of*
apelido [m.]; [BP] o sobrenome	*surname*
caravana [f.]	*caravan*
carro-cama [m.]	*campervan*
chegada [f.]	*arrival*
data [f.]	*date*
Em que nome?	*In what name?*
Faz favor de . . .	*Please . . .*
ficha [f.]	*form*
já está	*it's done, there*
local de nascimento [m.] also o lugar de nascimento	*place of birth*
nascimento [m.]	*birth*
nome [m.]	*first name*
parque [m.]	*park, campsite*
preencher	*to fill in*
receção [f.]; [BP] a recepção	*the reception (desk)*
reservado	*reserved*
tenda [f.]	*tent*
um lugar	*a place*
vaga [f.]	*pitch/site*

🔘 Diálogo

CUSTOMER: Bom dia. Temos um lugar reservado.

RECEPTIONIST: Em que nome?

CUSTOMER: Brown.

RECEPTIONIST: Ah, sim, aqui está. Vocês têm tenda, caravana, ou carro-cama?

CUSTOMER: Uma caravana e uma tenda.

RECEPTIONIST: Está bem. O número da vaga é o vinte e dois. Fica à esquerda, ao fundo do parque. Agora, faz favor de preencher esta ficha.

CUSTOMER: Claro. O que precisa saber?

RECEPTIONIST: O seu nome, apelido, número do passaporte, local e data de nascimento, a sua morada, e a data de chegada ao parque.

CUSTOMER: Já está.

RECEPTIONIST: A receção fecha às dez e meia da noite e abre às sete horas da manhã.

CUSTOMER: Obrigado.

ATIVIDADE
27·1

Fill in the form with the appropriate pieces of information.

dos Santos Pereira   Rua S. Pedro, 10, 3º esq, Braga   português
Castelo Branco   B1 372201568BJL   terça-feira, 10 de junho de 2010
José   25 de março de 1963

Parque de Campismo Belavista

Nome _____

Apelido _____

Data de nascimento _____

Local de nascimento _____

Morada _____

Nº de passaporte/bilhete de identidade _____

Nacionalidade _____

Data de chegada _____

Listen to someone checking in at a campsite. Look at the plan of the site below, and mark on it where they are placed, and whether they have a tent (T), caravan (C), or campervan (CV).

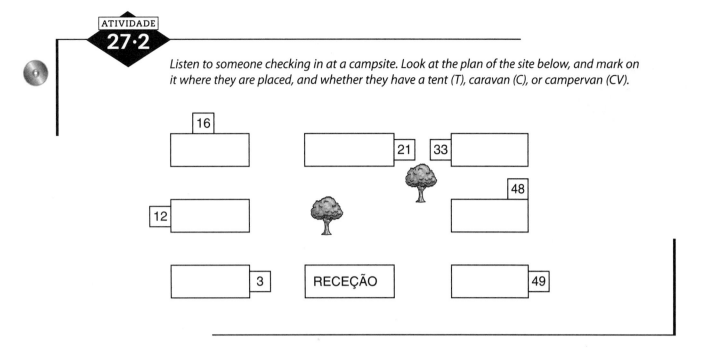

Somebody will ask you for some personal information. Try to answer each question in a natural way. Speak in the pauses on the recording.

Língua

When addressing more than one person, in less formal situations, an alternative to **os senhores/ as senhoras** is **vocês** (*you* plural). You can, of course, simply use the plural verb form, as you have seen in recent units, but as that form is also used for *they,* the use of **vocês** makes it clear who is doing the action. The singular equivalent is **você**, which is used widely throughout Brazil and by many people in Portugal.

De interesse

In Portugal and Brazil each person has an ID card, **um bilhete de identidade (BI)**.

Travel

A coach journey

VOCABULÁRIO

a próxima [f.]	*the next one*
breve	*short, brief*
camioneta [f.]; [BP] um ônibus	*a coach*
(*see* **De interesse**)	
chega	*(it) arrives*
de 30 em 30 minutos	*every 30 minutes*
de meia em meia hora	*every half an hour*
É direta?	*Is it direct?*
mudar	*to change*
partem	*they depart*
tem de *also* **tem que**	*you have to*
uma paragem	*a rest, stop*

💿 Diálogo

TRAVELER: A que horas há uma camioneta para Évora?

TICKET CLERK: As camionetas para Évora partem de trinta em trinta minutos.

TRAVELER: Bom, de meia em meia hora. E a que horas parte a próxima?

TICKET CLERK: A próxima para Évora parte às dezassete e vinte e cinco.

TRAVELER: É direta?

TICKET CLERK: Não. A senhora tem de mudar em Portalegre. A camioneta chega às dezoito e quarenta e cinco. Há uma breve paragem de quinze minutos. Parte às dezanove horas e chega a Évora às vinte e trinta.

TRAVELER: Então, queria um bilhete de ida e volta, se faz favor.

TICKET CLERK: Aqui só pode comprar a ida. O bilhete de volta tem de comprar lá, antes de viajar.

Fill in the blanks in this exercise using the timetable to guide you. The first one has been done for you.

CAMIONETAS PARA

Braga	8:00	8:45	9:30	10:15	11:00	11:45	12:30	13:15	14:00	14:45
Évora	8:15	8:30	8:45	9:00	9:15	9:30	9:45	10:00	10:15	10:30
Lisboa	8:25	8:50	9:15	9:40	10:05	10:30	10:55	11:20	11:45	12:10
Porto	8:30	9:20	10:10	11:00	11:50	12:40	13:30	14:20	15:10	16:00

1. As camionetas para o Porto partem de *cinquenta* em *cinquenta* minutos.

2. As camionetas para Évora partem de _____ em _____ minutos.

3. As camionetas para _____ partem de vinte e cinco em vinte e cinco minutos.

4. As camionetas para _____ partem de quarenta e cinco em quarenta e cinco minutos.

Listen to a dialogue about a coach journey and fill in the table below with any missing information.

DESTINATION	HOW OFTEN	NEXT DEPARTURE	CHANGE	ARRIVAL AT DESTINATION
_____	_____	_____	_____	_____

Now take part in a short listening and speaking activity based on the earlier dialogue. Supply your part of the dialogue by following the two prompts below and write the answers you are given on the recording.

1. (say) What time is there a coach to Viana?

   RESPONSE: _____

2. (say) Is it direct?

   RESPONSE: _____

Língua

Ter de/que + infinitive means *to have to* (the verb **ter** means *to have*).

Temos de comprar vinho.	*We have to buy wine.*
Tenho que visitar Portugal.	*I have to visit Portugal.*

De interesse

When travelling by bus, or coach, you will usually only be able to buy single tickets. So you must allow time before your return to buy another ticket. All travel in Portugal is extremely cheap and there are luxury **rápido-expresso** coaches between the main cities, from Oporto down through Lisbon and to Faro in the Algarve. All long-distance travel in Brazil is by bus/coach (sometimes for more than a day!), as there is very little rail infrastructure. The main types of tickets include **comum** (normal), **executivo** (more comfortable) and **leito** (often with reclining seats and on-board facilities).

Directions

Getting to the right platform

VOCABULÁRIO	
assim	*in that way, and so*
bilheteira [f.]; [BP] a bilheteria	*ticket office*
consigo	*with you*
continue	*continue*
desça	*go down*
escadas [f., pl.]	*steps*
espere	*wait*
fácil	*easy*
gentil	*kind*
já	*already*
lá em cima	*up there*
Ora essa!	*The very idea, come off it!*
Para chegar lá?	*To get there? (How does one get there?)*
passarela [f.]	*footbridge*
passe (por)	*pass (by, through, over)*
perdido/a	*lost*
sai	*(it) leaves*
Sempre em frente.	*Right/Straight ahead.*
suba	*go up*
tome	*take*
um momento	*a moment*
Vamos?	*Shall we go?/ Let's go?*
vire	*turn*

Diálogo

VISITOR: Desculpe. O comboio para Faro sai de que linha?

MAN: Da linha número três.

VISITOR: E para chegar lá?

MAN: Pois, suba estas escadas aqui, passe pela passarela lá em cima e desça até ao quiosque. Depois, vire à esquerda, continue sempre em frente até à bilheteira e tome a primeira à . . .

VISITOR: Espere um momento, já estou perdida!

MAN: Então vou lá consigo. Assim é mais fácil.

VISITOR: O senhor é muito gentil.

MAN: Ora essa! Vamos?

Match the pictures to the directions.

1.

a. passe

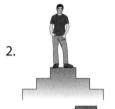

2.

b. suba

3.

c. desça

4.

d. lá em cima

5.

e. continue sempre em frente

Listen to someone being given instructions to get to the correct platform. Write the directions you hear and the correct platform number.

Directions: _____

_____

Platform number: _____

Now take part in a dialogue at a station. You want to know where the train for Braga leaves from. Follow the prompts below and see if you fully understand all the directions you are given.

1. From which platform does the train to Braga leave?

2. How do I get there?

3. Hang on a second. I'm already lost!

4. You're very kind, thank you.

Língua

When giving someone directions, you can tell them what to do in a couple of ways: by saying *you do this* as a suggestion, or simply *do this* as a polite command. When making a suggestion, say **o senhor/a senhora** or **você**. When making a command, there is no *you*.

		Suggestion		Command	
passar	*to pass*	**passa**	*you pass*	**passe!**	*pass!*
virar	*to turn*	**vira**	*you turn*	**vire!**	*turn!*
continuar	*to continue*	**continua**	*you continue*	**continue!**	*continue!*
tomar	*to take*	**toma**	*you take*	**tome!**	*take!*
esperar	*to wait/for*	**espera**	*you wait*	**espere!**	*wait!*
entrar	*to enter*	**entra**	*you enter*	**entre!**	*enter!*
descer	*to go down*	**desce**	*you go down*	**desça!**	*go down!*
ir	*to go*	**vai**	*you go*	**vá!**	*go!*
subir	*to go up*	**sobe**	*you go up*	**suba!**	*go up!*
seguir	*to carry on*	**segue**	*you carry on*	**siga!**	*carry on!*
sair	*to leave*	**sai**	*you leave*	**saia!**	*leave!*

De interesse

Most train stations in Portugal, however small they are, have a bar or cafe serving hot and cold drinks, and snacks for your journey. Toilets, on the other hand, are rather more hit and miss; quite often they are closed and facilities can be very basic. Most long-distance travel in Brazil is done by coach or air. However, there are a few rail journeys for train fans, including a couple of steam rides, on trains known as a **Maria Fumaça** (*Smoking Mary*). Good guide books or Internet sites have the relevant details.

Town amenities

At the post office

VOCABULÁRIO	
cabine [f.]	*telephone booth*
chamada [f.]	*phone call*
chamada a cobrar	*reverse charge (call)*
chamadas internacionais	*international calls*
Com quem?	*With whom?*
indicativo [m.]; [BP] o código	*code*
Não desligue.	*Don't hang up.*
no destino	*at the receiving end (destination)*
país [m.]	*country*
Qual . . .?	*Which/what . . .?*
Que . . .?	*What . . .?*
selo [m.]	*a stamp*
telefone [m.]	*telephone*

Diálogo

CUSTOMER: Queria fazer uma chamada.

ASSISTANT: Pode entrar na cabine três.

OPERATOR: Chamadas internacionais, bom dia.

CUSTOMER: Queria fazer uma chamada a cobrar no destino.

OPERATOR: Para que país?

CUSTOMER: Inglaterra.

OPERATOR: Qual é o indicativo da cidade?

CUSTOMER: É zero, um, cinco, dois, quatro.

OPERATOR: E o número do telefone?

CUSTOMER: É quatro, dois, um, cinco, zero, seis.

OPERATOR: Com quem quer falar?

CUSTOMER: Com a senhora White.

OPERATOR: E qual é o seu nome?

CUSTOMER: David White.

OPERATOR: Está bem. Só um momento—não desligue.

*Buying stamps: To ask how much a stamp costs, say **Quanto custa um selo**? To state which country you need it for, use **para** and the name of the country—**para a Inglaterra** (for England) or **para os Estados Unidos** (for the U.S.). Then use **queria** (I would like) to state how many, for example, **Queria dez se faz favor**.*

Now, match up the sets of stamps bought to the total amounts. Write the full amounts in Portuguese.

1. 10 x

2. 7 x

3. 4 x

4. 5 x

5. 2 x

a. Trezentos cêntimos

b. Oitocentos e cinquenta cêntimos

c. Duzentos cêntimos

d. Quatrocentos e vinte cêntimos

e. Trezentos e trinta e cinco cêntimos

ATIVIDADE 30·2

Listen to someone making an international call via an operator and fill in the table below with their details.

COUNTRY	LOCAL CODE	TELEPHONE	WANTS TO SPEAK TO
___	___	___	___

ATIVIDADE 30·3

Now practice making an international call yourself. Use the dialogue on the CD to guide you, and speak in the pauses, giving your own details.

Língua

Many question words (known as interrogatives) in Portuguese begin with **qu**. You already know these:

quem	*who*
qual	*which/what*
(o) que	*what*
quando	*when*
quanto	*how much*

De interesse

Making phone calls in Portugal is very expensive, be it from **uma cabine telefónica** in the street, from the **os correios** (*post office*), or from the **Telecomunicações Portuguesas** (*Telecom offices*). phone cards are widespread. You can buy the cards where you see the sign **Cartão Credifone**.

In Brazil, the shape of on-street phone booths resembles a huge ear, hence their nickname **orelhão** (*big ear*).

Portuguese and Brazilians are avid mobile-phone users; the word for *cell phone* is **telemóvel** and in Brazil **celular**.

Downtown

Shopping at the market

31

VOCABULÁRIO

A como é . . . ?	*What price is . . . ?*
alface [f.]	*lettuce*
batatas [f., pl.]	*potatoes*
cenouras [f., pl.]	*carrots*
cogumelos [m., pl.]	*mushrooms*
couve-flor [f.]	*cauliflower*
dê-me; [BP] me dê/me dá	*give me*
gramas [m., pl.]	*grams*
laranjas [f., pl.]	*oranges*
maçãs [f., pl.]	*apples*
maduro	*ripe*
meio quilo	*half a kilo*
melão [m.]	*melon*
pera [f.]	*pear*
Que mais?	*What else?*
tomates [m., pl.]	*tomatoes*
um quilo	*a kilo*

Diálogo

CUSTOMER: Bom dia, senhora. Tem tomates hoje?

VENDOR: Tenho, sim. Quantos quer? Estão muito bons hoje.

CUSTOMER: Dê-me um quilo dos mais maduros.

VENDOR: Mais alguma coisa?

CUSTOMER: Também queria um quilo de maçãs, cinco quilos de
batatas, e dois de laranjas.

VENDOR: Que mais?

CUSTOMER: Tem couve-flor?

VENDOR: Hoje não. Tenho cogumelos e cenouras.

CUSTOMER: Dê-me duzentos e cinquenta gramas de cogumelos,
se faz favor. Ah, e uma alface.

VENDOR: Mais?

CUSTOMER: A como é a pera?

VENDOR: A trezentos o quilo.

CUSTOMER: Então dê-me meio quilo e também um melão, obrigado.

ATIVIDADE 31·1

Match the captions to the pictures.

1. um quilo de cenouras

a.

2. meio quilo de tomates

b.

3. duas alfaces

c.

4. duzentos e cinquenta gramas de cogumelos

d.

5. dois quilos de batatas

e.

ATIVIDADE 31·2

Look at the list of market stand produce below, then listen to someone buying fruit and vegetables from it. Put a check mark for anything they buy, and write down how much they take. Put a cross for anything not available today.

1. tomatoes _____

2. potatoes _____

3. apples _____

4. oranges _____

5. cauliflower _____

6. mushrooms _____

7. carrots _____

8. lettuce _____

9. pears _____

10. melons _____

11. leeks _____

12. grapes _____

13. bananas _____

14. onions _____

15. plums _____

ATIVIDADE
31·3

Now see if you can do your market shopping successfully. Take part in the dialogue, using the following prompts to guide you.

1. Good morning. Do you have any mushrooms today?

2. I'll have 250g.

3. I'd also like ½ kg of pears, 3 lettuces, and 6 kg of potatoes.

4. Do you have melon?

5. Well, then, give me a kilo of apples.

6. How much are the oranges today?

7. Give me 2 kg, thank you.

Língua

If metric weights confuse you, the following approximations might help when you are buying foodstuffs.

2½ kg	5 lbs
1 kg	2 lbs
½ kg	1 lb
250g	½ lb
100g	¼ lb

To ask how much a product costs today, use **a como é o/a . . .?** The answer will be **a . . . o quilo**, ie., *X* euros/reais *the kilo*, not *a kilo*.

To say *of the best/ripest/cheapest*, etc., remember the contracted forms **dos** and **das** you learned in Unit 5:

de + os → dos
de + as → das

um quilo dos mais baratos *a kilo of the cheapest* (lit. *a kilo of the more cheap*)

De interesse

Fresh fruit and vegetables are very cheap in Portugal, especially when bought at the **mercado**. Try the delicious oranges, tasty tomatoes, and refreshing melons. Brazilian tropical fruit is an absolute must when you are there: fresh **maracujá** (*passion fruit*), **manga** (*mango*) or **goiaba** (*guava*) are delicious.

Personal choices

What would you like to do?

VOCABULÁRIO	
(eu) sei	*I know*
(eu) sempre quis	*I've always wanted*
(tu) gostarias	*you (fam.) would like*
amanhã	*tomorrow*
bar [m.]	*bar*
boate [f.] *also* **uma discoteca**	*nightclub*
comigo	*with me*
Concordas?	*(Do) you (fam.) agree?*
Concordo.	*I agree.*
em casa	*at home*
fechado(s)	*closed*
feriado [m.]	*national holiday/bank holiday*
Fica combinado.	*That's decided then.*
filme [m.]	*film*
fora	*out, outside*
gostaria	*I (he/she/you) would like*
já que	*given that, as*
jantamos	*we dine*
jantar	*to dine*
mais tarde	*later*
nesse caso [m.]	*in that case*
O que (é que) . . .?	*What (is it that) . . .?*
passear	*to stroll, wander*
podemos	*we can*
por fim	*finally*
preferia	*I (he/she/you) would prefer*
preferias	*you (fam.) would prefer*
relaxar	*to relax*
Tens razão.	*You're (fam.) right.*

Diálogo

MARIA: Então, João, o que é que tu gostarias de fazer amanhã?

JOÃO: Bom, já que amanhã é feriado, gostaria de ir ver um filme
ao cinema, depois jantar fora, e por fim relaxar num bar.

MARIA: Não preferias visitar o Museu dos Coches comigo?
Eu sempre quis ir.

João: Todos os museus estão fechados nos feriados.

Maria: Tens razão. Nesse caso preferia passear pela avenida, tomar uma bebida, e depois passar a noite numa boate.

João: Eu sei! Por que não jantamos em casa, depois vamos passear na avenida até ao Tivoli, e mais tarde vamos ao T' Clube? Podemos ir ao museu no sábado. Concordas?

Maria: Concordo.

João: Bem, então, fica combinado.

ATIVIDADE 32·1

Fill in the gaps in this exercise with these words:

ver   passar   jantar   ir   tomamos   boate   cinema   museu   bar

1. Gostaria de ir ao _____ para _____ um filme.

2. Vamos a um _____ e _____ uma bebida.

3. Preferia _____ em casa.

4. Gostarias de _____ ao _____ amanhã?

5. Podemos _____ a noite numa _____.

ATIVIDADE 32·2

Listen to Paula and Eduardo talking about what they would like to do on the weekend, and mark their preferences in the table below.

	EDUARDO		PAULA	
	Sat	Sun	Sat	Sun
see a film	_____	_____	_____	_____
eat out	_____	_____	_____	_____
eat in	_____	_____	_____	_____
visit a museum	_____	_____	_____	_____
go dancing	_____	_____	_____	_____
relax in a bar	_____	_____	_____	_____
stroll in the center	_____	_____	_____	_____

Look at the table below for choices of activities for different days of the week, and use it to answer the questions on the recording, about what you would like to do.

Monday	Tuesday	Wednesday
Thursday	Friday	Saturday

Língua

For talking about preferences, you will need the following verb forms:

		I	*you (fam.)*	*he/she/you (pol)*	*we*	*they/you (pl.)*
gostar	*to like*	**gostaria**	**gostarias**	**gostaria**	**gostaríamos**	**gostariam**
preferir	*to prefer*	**preferiria**	**preferirias**	**preferiria**	**preferiríamos**	**prefeririam**

In everyday Portuguese, especially in Portugal, two alternative forms of these verbs are used: **gostava/gostavas/gostava/gostávamos/gostavam**, and **preferia/preferias/preferia/preferíamos/preferiam**, as used in the dialogue. These are certainly easier to say than the longer form **preferiria**, etc. You will come across these verb forms again later in the course, as they actually belong to a tense called the imperfect.

De interesse

Some of the places mentioned in the dialogue are worth visiting if you are in Lisbon. **O Museu dos Coches** (*carriage museum*), full of beautiful coaches and carriages, is situated downriver, in a part of Lisbon known as **Belém** (*Bethlehem*). In the center of Lisbon, you can walk down the **Avenida da Liberdade**, the main artery of the city, to the river **Tejo** (*Tagus*), and visit the **Tivoli** cinema halfway down. In the Brazilian city of Belém, way up in the Amazon, the building not to miss is the **Teatro da Paz** theater and opera house, built around 1870 when the region was riding the wave of the rubber boom.

Vacations

Discussing next year's holidays

VOCABULÁRIO	
amigos [m., pl.]	friends
aprender a	to learn (how) to
biblioteca [f.]	library
Boa sorte!	Good luck!
cão [m.]; [BP] o cachorro	dog
cerâmica [f.]	pottery
cuidar de	to look after, take care of
deixe-me; [BP] me deixe	let me
espero	I hope
Holanda [f.]	Holland
imenso	a lot
levar	to take, carry
no ano que vem	next year
no próximo ano [m.]	next year
ótimo	great
Passou bem? (*colloquial* EP)	Are you well?
pelo menos	at least
pintar	to paint
pintura [f.]	painting
saco [m.]	(carrier) bag
trouxe	I (he/she/you) have brought
um curso	a course
um mês	a month
vai	(you/he/she/it) are/is going

Diálogo

JÚLIO: Olá, Maria. Passou bem?

MARIA: Sim, obrigada, Júlio, mas estou um pouco cansada por causa destes livros que trouxe da biblioteca.

JÚLIO: Deixe-me levar o seu saco, então. O que tem aqui? Livros sobre pintura; vai aprender a pintar?

MARIA: No ano que vem vou fazer um curso de verão sobre pintura e cerâmica.

JÚLIO: Onde?

MARIA: Na Holanda. Eu e o meu marido vamos lá passar as férias. Onde vai passar as férias no próximo ano, Júlio?

JÚLIO: Eu? Provavelmente vou visitar amigos no Brasil. Espero ficar pelo menos um mês no Rio.

MARIA: Ótimo! Vai gostar imenso. Mas a sua mulher vai também?

JÚLIO: Não, ela vai ficar em casa a cuidar do cão!

ATIVIDADE 33·1

Translate the sentences into Portuguese using the following words.

vou	vais	vai	vamos	viajar	no mês que vem	na semana que vem
vão	ficar	ver	passear	visitar	no ano que vem	

1. We are going to Brazil next year.

_____ _____ o Brasil _____.

2. She is going to stay at home next week.

_____ _____ em casa _____.

3. Next month you (fam.) are going to see your friends.

_____ _____ _____ as tuas amigas.

4. I am going to travel to Holland next year.

_____ _____ à Holanda _____.

5. Next week they are going to stroll in town.

_____ _____ _____ na cidade.

ATIVIDADE 33·2

Listen to what two people are going to do during their holidays and fill in the table below with their details.

WHEN	WHAT	WHERE
1. _____	_____	_____
2. _____	_____	_____

Now take part in a dialogue about future vacations. Follow the prompts below and speak in the pauses.

1. Next year my family and I are going to visit Denmark in the winter.

2. Where are you going to spend your holidays next month?

3. Next month I'm going to stay at home and do a Portuguese course.

Língua

To express a future action, however close or remote it may be (this afternoon, tomorrow, next year etc.), the easiest way is to simply use part of the verb *to go* (**ir**), plus the verb representing the action to be taken, just as we do in English (for example, *I'm going to watch football*). You will need to know the appropriate forms of **ir**:

eu	vou	*I go/am going*
tu	vais	*you go/are going*
ele/ela/o senhor/a senhora/você	vai	*he/she/you go/is/are going*
nós	vamos	*we go/are going*
eles/elas/os senhores/as senhoras/vocês	vão	*they/you (pl.) go/are going*

Then, you will need a few expressions of future time, such as **o ano/o mês/a semana que vem** (*next year/month/week*), or even **em** (*in*) + months/seasons, or **às** (*at*) + time. For instance:

Eu vou passar férias no Japão **no ano que vem**. *I'm going on vacation (going to have a vacation) to Japan next year.*

Tu vais viajar **em janeiro**? *Are you going to travel in January?*
Maria vai ver um filme **às oito horas**. *Maria's going to see a film at eight o'clock.*

De interesse

Brazilians love travelling and many visit the UK every year, as well as other European countries and the USA. The Portuguese, on the other hand, often spend their holidays visiting family in Portugal, or having time on the beach, and with 800 km of fine coastline, that's not really surprising!

The weather

Weather reports

VOCABULÁRIO	
ar [m.]	*air*
fraco	*weak*
graus [m., pl.]	*degrees*
leste [m.]	*east*
mar [m.]	*sea*
menos	*minus*
moderado	*moderate*
norte [m.]	*north*
observada [f.]	*observed, noted*
oeste [m.]	*west*
ondulação [f.]	*tide (height)*
parcialmente	*partially*
Portugal continental	*mainland Portugal*
previsão [f.]	*forecast*
qualidade [f.]	*quality*
regiões [f., pl.]	*regions*
sair (de)	*to go out, leave (from)*
sul [m.]	*south*
televisão [f.]	*television*
temperatura [f.]	*temperature*
últimas [f., pl.]	*last, past*

Diálogo

MAN: Vamos ver a previsão do tempo na televisão antes de sair.

WEATHER PRESENTER: E agora temos a previsão do tempo para hoje em todo Portugal continental: nas regiões do norte e do centro, o céu vai estar pouco nublado, com vento fraco do leste. No sul, o céu vai estar parcialmente nublado com vento moderado. As temperaturas vão chegar a quinze graus no norte, e dezassete no sul. No oeste, o mar vai ter uma ondulação de dois a três metros. A qualidade do ar observada em Lisboa nas últimas vinte e quatro horas é razoável.

MAN: Vamos ficar em casa?

*Read the weather report again, and write if these statements are **verdadeiro** or **falso**.*

1. Na região do norte vai ter vento do oeste.   _____

2. No sul a temperatura vai chegar a 17°.   _____

3. Lisboa tem boa qualidade de ar.   _____

4. O vento vai estar moderado na região central.   _____

5. A ondulação do mar vai chegar a três metros no oeste.   _____

Listen to a report on the temperatures in capital cities around the world, and complete the table below with the correct temperatures/cities. Some have already been done for you.

CITY	TEMPERATURE
Madrid	_____
London	_____
_____	8°
Amsterdam	_____
_____	14°

Now it's your turn to be the weather person on TV reading a weather report. Follow the prompts below.

1. Good evening. Here we have the weather forecast for today for England.

2. In the northern region the sky will be cloudy with a moderate wind.

3. The temperatures are going to reach 18° in the south.

4. The quality of air observed in London is reasonable.

Língua

Vamos . . ., as you learned in Unit 33, means *we're going to* . . . . It can also mean *shall we . . .?*, **Vamos sair?** (*Shall we go out?*)

It is also used with other verbs in the (basic form) infinitive, in the sense *let's* . . . : **Vamos ver** (*Let's see.*).

De interesse

Portugal continental is mainland Portugal. Usually, on weather forecasts on TV, radio, and in the newspapers, you will also be given information on **os Açores** (the Azorean Islands), and **Madeira**. These islands out in the Atlantic, are Portuguese territories.

·35· Ill health

Feeling ill

braço [m.]	arm
Caiu?	Have you fallen?/Did you fall?
cortei	I cut/I've cut
costas [f., pl.]	back
dedo [m.]	finger
dentes [m., pl.]	teeth
doem-me (pl.); [BP] me doem	. . . hurt
dói-me (sing); [BP] me dói	. . . hurts
estômago [m.]	stomach
hoje de manhã	this morning
Isto é grave.	This is serious.
Magoei; [BP/EP] *also* machuquei	I hurt/I've hurt
Não estou nada bem.	I'm not well at all.
Não me sinto bem.	I don't feel well.
Não sei.	I don't know.
o problema	the problem
O que tem feito?	What have you been doing?
olhos [m., pl.]	eyes
pé [m.]	foot
pernas [f., pl.]	legs
Que estranho!	How strange!
ter dores	to hurt (have pain)

 Diálogo

MAN: Não me sinto bem.

DOCTOR: Qual é o problema?

MAN: Tenho dores nas costas e nas pernas.

DOCTOR: Caiu?

MAN: Não. Não sei o que é. Dói-me o braço, e o estômago.

DOCTOR: Que estranho. Isto é grave. Tem dor de cabeça?

MAN: Não, de cabeça não, mas doem-me os dentes e os olhos.
Não estou nada bem.

DOCTOR: Mas o que tem feito?

MAN: Cortei o dedo ontem, e magoei o pé hoje de manhã.
  Ai, que dor!

DOCTOR: Seria melhor ir para a cama.

ATIVIDADE

35·1

Match the captions to the parts of the body by drawing lines.

1. Dói-me o braço.

2. Dói-me o pé.

3. Me doem os olhos.

4. Dói-me o estômago.

5. Doem-me os dentes.

ATIVIDADE

35·2

Listen to someone talking about their ailments and write in the table below what is wrong with them.

HAS A PAIN IN . . .

leg	arm	eyes	head
____	____	____	____

HAS CUT . . .

foot	leg	arm
____	____	____

HAS HURT . . .

leg	back
____	____

Take part in a dialogue yourself now. Imagine you have various ailments and need to tell a doctor or pharmacist about them. Follow the prompts below.

1. Hello. I don't feel very well.

2. I have a headache and my teeth hurt.

3. Yesterday I hurt my head and cut my finger.

4. Not in my eyes, but my stomach aches.

Língua

Note the position of the pronouns **me/se** in the different sentences below:

Dói-**me**	*. . . hurts me.*	Não **me** dói.	*It doesn't hurt me.*
Sinto-**me**	*I feel . . .*	Não **me** sinto bem.	*I don't feel well.*
Chamo-**me**	*I am called . . .*	Como **se** chama?	*What are you called?*

Usually, pronouns that are objects of a verb (ie., they receive the action of a verb) go after the verb, joined to it by a hyphen, but after negatives and question words, they move before the verb.

In Brazil, however, pronouns tend to appear before the verb whatever the circumstance: **Me sinto bem/eu me chamo . . .**

De interesse

Before you go to Portugal or Brazil, make sure you have adequate insurance to cover medical costs (doctor, hospital, dentist). Take your completed European Health card (the replacement for the E111 form), or your U.S. insurance documents and carry with you all medical documentation in reference to medication you may be taking.

Time

Discussing when things happened

36

VOCABULÁRIO

almoçar	*to have lunch*
barriga [f.]	*tummy/belly*
bebi	*I drank*
cedo	*early*
chegámos; [BP] chegamos	*we arrived*
cheguei	*I arrived*
começou	*(it) started*
comeu	*you (he/she/it) ate*
comi	*I ate*
cuidado com	*(take) care with/be careful with*
Era meia-noite.	*It was midnight.*
Eram nove e meia.	*It was half past nine.*
fez	*you (he/she/it) did, made*
fui	*I went*
ginástica [f.]	*aerobics*
indigestão [f.]	*indigestion*
logo	*then*
por volta de	*around, about*
saí	*I went out*
senhor(a) doutor(a)	*doctor (title)*
voltei	*I returned*

Diálogo

PATIENT: Ai, senhor doutor. Não me sinto nada bem.

DOCTOR: Qual é o problema?

PATIENT: Dói-me muito a barriga.

DOCTOR: Quando começou a dor?

PATIENT: Hoje de manhã por volta das nove horas.

DOCTOR: O que fez ontem?

PATIENT: Ontem, bem, de manhã fui para o trabalho cedo, voltei a casa ao meio-dia para almoçar, e saí logo para fazer ginástica.

DOCTOR: E à noite, comeu alguma coisa?

PATIENT: Pois sim, fui a um restaurante com uma amiga.

DOCTOR: A que horas?

PATIENT: Eram nove e meia quando lá chegámos. Eu comi arroz de marisco e pudim, e bebi meia garrafa de vinho. Era meia-noite quando cheguei a casa.

DOCTOR: Acho que a senhora tem indigestão. Cuidado com a comida!

ATIVIDADE 36·1

Match the captions below to the pictures opposite. In each one Paulo is saying what he did yesterday.

1. bebi vinho

a.

2. cheguei a casa

b.

3. almocei

c.

4. saí para o trabalho

d.

5. fui ao cinema

e.

ATIVIDADE
36·2

Listen to Ana saying what time she did things yesterday. Fill in the missing times below.

1. _____ went to work.

2. _____ returned home for lunch.

3. _____ went to a restaurant.

4. _____ arrived home.

ATIVIDADE
36·3

Now take part in a dialogue about what you did yesterday, using the prompts below to guide you.

1. Yesterday morning I went to work early and returned home for lunch at 1:30.

2. Then I left to go to the library.

3. I went to a restaurant with a friend.

4. I ate chicken, almond cake, and I drank half a bottle of white wine.

5. It was 11:15 when I arrived home.

Língua

Talking about things which have taken place in the past can be rather complex, so do not over-concern yourself with it at this stage. Two important things to remember:

◆ In Portuguese, questions in the past do not have a word corresponding to the English *did*, as in *what did you do?* You simply ask **O que fez?** (*what you did?*)

◆ When talking about time in the past, use **eram** when there is more than one hour involved, and **era** for one o'clock, midday, and midnight:

Eram cinco e meia.	*It was 5:30.*
Era uma menos dez.	*It was ten to one.*
Era meia-noite.	*It was midnight.*

Time: Discussing when things happened   **109**

De interesse

The Portuguese **vinho verde** (*green wine*) is a Portuguese speciality, young, fruity, and very enjoyable. In northern Portugal, where it is grown, you also come across the red version of it (**vinho verde tinto**), which is usually served chilled.

Brazil is not as renowned for its wine; the drinks of choice are **caipirinha** (a cocktail made from sugar cane alcohol, crushed lime, and sugar), **guaraná** (a sweet soft drink—the Brazilian Cola), or a wonderfully chilled draft beer—**um chope**.

People
Discussing jobs and professions

37

VOCABULÁRIO

Ainda são novos. [m., pl.]	*They are still young.*
cunhado, cunhada	*brother-in-law, sister-in-law*
desenhador(a)	*designer*
Diga-me.; [BP] Me diga.	*Tell me.*
empresa [f.]	*business*
era	*was/used to be*
escola [f.]	*school*
escritor(a)	*writer*
exporta	*(it) exports*
funcionário público [m.]	*civil servant*
informática [f.]	*IT (computers)*
juntos [m., pl.]	*together*
O [que é] que faz/fazem?	*What do you (pl.) (he/she/they) do?*
o trabalho	*the work*
portanto	*therefore*
primo/a	*cousin*
professor(a)	*teacher*
reformado; [BP] aposentado	*retired*
secretária [f.]	*secretary*
sobrinho, sobrinha	*nephew, niece*
trabalha	*he/she (it/you) works*
trabalham	*they (you pl.) work*
trabalho	*I work*

Diálogo

ANTÓNIO: Diga-me uma coisa, Anne; o que é que faz?

ANNE: Eu? Pois sou professora. Trabalho numa escola primária.

ANTÓNIO: Gosta do trabalho?

ANNE: Gosto sim. O meu pai também era professor, mas agora é reformado. A minha mãe é secretária.

ANTÓNIO: E o que fazem os seus irmãos?

ANNE: Bom. O meu irmão trabalha com a informática numa empresa internacional nos Estados Unidos, e a minha irmã é escritora. O meu cunhado é desenhador, portanto os dois trabalham juntos.

111

ANTÓNIO: E os seus sobrinhos? Trabalham?

ANNE: Não, ainda são novos. E o António? O que faz?

ANTÓNIO: Eu trabalho com o meu primo. Temos uma pequena empresa que exporta vinhos para a Alemanha.

ATIVIDADE 37·1

Who does which job? Link up the Portuguese statements on the left with the correct English versions on the right. There is one extra English sentence.

1. Sou professora.

2. A minha prima é secretária.

3. O João trabalha com a informática.

4. O meu irmão é desenhador.

a. My cousin is a secretary.

b. My sister is a designer.

c. I am a teacher.

d. John works with computers.

e. My brother is a designer.

ATIVIDADE 37·2

Listen to three people being interviewed about their jobs and fill in the table below with their details. Some have been done for you.

NAME	PROFESSION	PLACE OF WORK
1. José _____	_____	_____
2. _____	_____	_____
3. _____	civil servant	_____

ATIVIDADE 37·3

Now you will play the role of Jorge Santos in a dialogue on the recording. You may need to revisit Unit 25 for the names of relations.

1. Good afternoon, Teresa.

2. I'm a designer. I work for an international company in Lisbon.

3. Yes, I like it a lot.

4. My wife works in a school. She's a secretary.

5. What do you do, Teresa?

Língua

You have already learned the verb **gostar** (*to like*). Note that it always requires the preposition **de** when it is followed by an object or a verb. You have probably noticed that **de** also contracts with **um/uma** and **este/esta** (*this*), **aquele/aquela** (*that*), for example:

Gosto do bolo.	*I like the cake.*
O Manuel não **gosta duns** vinhos.	*Manuel doesn't like some wines.*
Gostas desta camisa?	*Do you like this blouse?*
Não **gostamos daquelas** praias.	*We don't like those beaches.*

When asking simply, *Do you like?*, **de** is not needed: **Gosta?** The answer will then be just **gosto** (*I like*) or **não gosto** (*I don't like*).

The preposition **em** (*in/on*) also contracts with the same words above (**um**, **este**, **aquele**, etc.), the **em** becoming an **n** that is placed at the beginning of each word, thus:

Trabalho **numa** fábrica.	*I work in a factory.*
Vivo **naquele** apartamento.	*I live in that apartment.*

De interesse

As Latin countries, both Portugal and Brazil have had traditional roles for women as the mainstay of the family and house. It is still the case with older generations, but in modern society in these countries, women are now competing more favorably with their male counterparts and most younger women go out to work.

Eating out

Asking about what's on the menu

VOCABULÁRIO	
açorda de marisco [f.]	*thick bread soup with seafood*
alérgico a	*allergic to*
alho [m.]	*garlic*
as nossas [f., pl.]	*our*
azeitonas [f., pl.]	*olives*
bacalhau na cataplana [m.]	*cod cooked in a cataplana (see* De interesse*)*
bastante	*quite, enough*
batatas fritas [f., pl.]	*chips/fries*
cebola [f.]	*onion*
contém	*(it) contains*
dá	*is enough (lit.* it gives*)*
feijão [m.]	*beans*
feijoada transmontana [f.]	*bean stew from Trás-os-Montes (northern Portugal)*
feito	*made*
fruta da época [f.]	*fruit of the season*
Já escolheram?	*Have you (pl.) chosen yet?*
meia dose [f.]	*half a portion, helping*
pimentão [m.]	*green pepper*
porção [f.]	*portion*
porções [f., pl.]	*portions*
prato [m.]	*dish, plate*
queijo da serra [m.]	*Serra cheese (Portuguese mountain)*
saber	*to know a fact, how to do something*
se quiser	*if you wish/want*
traga	*bring*
uma dose	*a portion, helping*
vêm	*they come*

 ## Diálogo

WAITER: Já escolheram?

CUSTOMER: Sim. Queríamos uma açorda de marisco e uma feijoada transmontana. Uma coisa—meia dose dá para uma pessoa?

WAITER: Dá sim. As nossas porções são bastante grandes.

CUSTOMER: Então, só meia dose da feijoada. Outra coisa, o meu marido é alérgico a cebolas, e queria saber como é feito o bacalhau na cataplana.

WAITER: Bom, este prato contém bacalhau (claro!), azeitonas, tomate, alho, pimentão e cebola; mas podemos fazer sem cebola se quiser.

CUSTOMER: Está bem. Os pratos vêm com salada ou legumes?

WAITER: A feijoada vem com arroz, e os outros com batatas fritas e salada.

CUSTOMER: Então traga uma dose de legumes também, faz favor.

WAITER: Muito bem. Vão querer sobremesa?

CUSTOMER: Sim. Queremos a fruta da época, e uma porção do queijo da serra. Obrigada.

ATIVIDADE 38·1

Fill in the gaps in this text with appropriate Portuguese words or phrases.

(*We would like*) _____ bacalhau na cataplana, com batatas fritas e (*salad*) _____ A minha mulher queria (*a half-serving*) _____ da feijoada com (*rice*) _____. (*Bring*) _____ uma dose de legumes também, se faz favor. Para (*dessert*) _____ queríamos (*fruit*) _____ da época, e dois (*small black coffees*) _____.

ATIVIDADE 38·2

Joan is allergic to tomatoes. Listen to descriptions of what is in two dishes, checking off the list below. You can then decide which of the two she can eat. You may need to review Unit 31.

INGREDIENTS	DISH 1	DISH 2		DISH 1	DISH 2
rice	___	___	onion	___	___
garlic	___	___	olive	___	___
tomato	___	___	pork	___	___
green pepper	___	___	cod	___	___
carrot	___	___			

Now you will take part in a dialogue with a waiter about different dishes. Follow the prompts below.

1. Yes, we would like the cataplana cod and a bean stew.

2. Is a half-portion enough for one person?

3. In that case, only a half-portion of the cod.

4. Do the dishes come with chips or salad?

5. In that case, please bring a salad as well.

Língua

Se quiser, meaning *if you like/want,* is used in many situations in everyday Portuguese. For example, if someone says to you **Vamos ao cinema?** (*Shall we go to the cinema?*) you could say **se quiser** (*if you like/want to*), or if you are talking to more than one person, **se quiserem**.

De interesse

It is quite acceptable to order **meia dose** (*half a helping*) in Portugal, especially of the more filling dishes. Many menus have a separate price listed for half-helpings. A **cataplana** is a round, copper vessel of Moorish origin which works like a pressure cooker, and captures the full flavour of food cooked in it.

An interesting style of restaurant in Brazil is the **gaucho** (*cowboy*)-inspired **churrascaria-rodízio**, a sort of barbecue house. There is a self-service salad bar, and waiters constantly circulate with hot cooked meats on large skewers or even swords, serving you with your choice of meat whenever you indicate you want more!

Accommodations

Inside a house

VOCABULÁRIO	
à frente	*at the front*
aqui em cima	*up here*
bem em frente	*right in front*
casa [f.]	*house*
cozinha [f.]	*kitchen*
creio (que)	*I believe (that)*
deixe	*leave*
dentro	*inside*
em baixo	*downstairs*
em cima	*upstairs*
entrada [f.]	*entrance/hall*
Entre!	*Enter/Come in!*
estadia [f.]	*stay*
infelizmente	*unfortunately*
jardim [m.]	*garden*
junto com	*together with*
lá em baixo	*down there*
mala [f.]	*suitcase*
mesmo	*same*
porta [f.]	*door*
quintal [m.]	*yard*
sala (de estar) [f.]	*living room*
sala de jantar [f.]	*dining room*
separado	*separate*
subir	*to go up(stairs)*
tomamos	*we have/take (meals)*
venha	*come*
viu	*you (he/she/it) saw*

🔘 Diálogo

SRA OLIVEIRA: Olá, e bem-vindo à nossa casa.

CHARLES: Obrigado. Creio que vou gostar muito da minha estadia aqui.

SRA OLIVEIRA: Entre, faz favor. Deixe a mala aqui na entrada e venha ver a casa.

CHARLES: Está bem.

SRA OLIVEIRA: Aqui à esquerda tem a sala de estar junto com uma sala de jantar. Geralmente tomamos o pequeno almoço aqui na cozinha, à sua direita. Fora da casa há um quintal.

CHARLES: Não tem jardim?

SRA OLIVEIRA: Só aquele que o Charles viu à frente da casa. Vamos subir? . . . Aqui em cima há três quartos—o nosso, o do nosso filho, e este, onde o Charles vai ficar. Infelizmente não tem casa de banho dentro do mesmo quarto, mas há uma em frente, aqui, nesta porta. Lá em baixo há um W.C. separado, à direita.

ATIVIDADE 39·1

Match the Portuguese room names to the English ones.

1. a sala de estar
2. o quarto (de dormir)
3. a cozinha
4. o jardim
5. a casa de banho/ o banheiro
6. a sala de jantar

a. the kitchen
b. the bedroom
c. the dining room
d. the garden
e. the living room
f. the bathroom

ATIVIDADE 39·2

You will hear someone describing their house as they show you around. Listen to their description and write the names of the rooms numbered on the plans below.

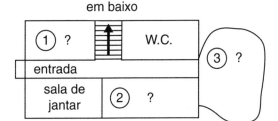
em baixo

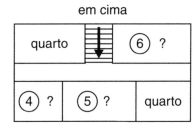
em cima

*Using the **Língua** section below, work out the Portuguese for the following, and say your answers in the pauses on the recording.*

1. my bedrooms

2. your (fam.) house

3. your (polite) garden

4. your (polite) kitchens

5. his living room

6. her dining room

Língua

So far you have come across isolated examples of the words for *my, his, your,* etc. Here is a simplified table of all the forms you may have encountered so far:

	Singular		Plural	
	Masculine	**Feminine**	**Masculine**	**Feminine**
my	(o) meu	(a) minha	(os) meus	(as) minhas
your (fam.)	(o) teu	(a) tua	(os) teus	(as) tuas
your (pol.)	(o) seu	(a) sua	(os) seus	(as) suas
our	(o) nosso	(a) nossa	(os) nossos	(as) nossas
his	o . . . dele	a . . . dele	os . . . dele	as . . . dele
her	o . . . dela	a . . . dela	os . . . dela	as . . . dela
their	o . . . deles/as	a . . . deles/as	os . . . deles/as	as . . . deles/as

Remember that the word you choose from the table depends on whether the possessed article is masculine or feminine, and singular or plural.

a minha filha	*my daughter*
os seus filhos	*your children*
o meu filho	*my son*
as suas irmãs	*your sisters*

It is also possible to use the forms **seu/sua/seus/suas** for *his, her* and *their,* providing there is no ambiguity about the statement. Hence, **o seu carro** could mean *his/her/your/their car,* unless the context gives you more details.

De interesse

Casa in Portuguese means both *house* and *home* (also translated as the word **lar**). Many Portuguese and Brazilian people refer to their **casa**, although it is more likely to be an apartment, either in an old downtown traditional building, or in a modern block on the outskirts.

Travel

A visit to a petrol/gasoline station

40

VOCABULÁRIO

(um) litro e meio	*one and a half liters*
adeus	*goodbye*
bomba de gasolina [f.]	*gasoline pump*
depósito [m.]	*tank*
encha	*fill (command)*
estação de serviço [f.]	*service station*
Fica a . . .	*It is at a distance of . . .*
gasóleo [m.]; [BP] o diesel	*diesel*
gasolina [f.]; [BP] *also* **o combustível**	*gas*
normal	*normal/2-star*
oficina de automóveis [f.]	*garage/repair garage*
pneus [m., pl.]	*tyres*
posto de gasolina [m.]	*small petrol station*
pressão [f.]	*(air) pressure*
pronto	*right then, ready*
sem chumbo	*unleaded*
super	*4-star (see De interesse for gasoline terms)*
um litro	*a liter*
um mapa	*a map*
uns . . . quilómetros; **[BP] quilômetros**	*some . . . kilometers*
vai ter de/que	*you're going to have to*
vendemos	*we sell*
verificar	*to check*

🖸 Diálogo

DRIVER: Olá, bom dia. Encha o depósito, por favor.

ATTENDANT: Quer super ou normal?

DRIVER: Super, se faz favor, mas tem gasolina sem chumbo?

ATTENDANT: Temos sem, senhora.

DRIVER: Então, queria sem chumbo.

ATTENDANT: Pronto.

DRIVER: Tem óleo?

ATTENDANT: Temos. O que quer? Um litro? Litro e meio . . . ?

DRIVER: Pode ser um litro. E tem mapas da região?

ATTENDANT: Não vendemos mapas. A senhora vai ter de comprar um na cidade mais: próxima.

DRIVER: É longe daqui?

ATTENDANT: Fica a uns dez quilómetros daqui.

DRIVER: Obrigada. Vou verificar a água e a pressão dos pneus também.

ATIVIDADE 40·1

Match the Portuguese and English sentences. There are two extra English statements.

1. dois litros de óleo
2. vinte e oito euros
3. dez litros de gasolina
4. cinco litros de gasóleo
5. quarenta e seis reais

a. five liters of diesel
b. two liters of gasoline
c. 46 Reals
d. ten liters of gasoline
e. two liters of oil
f. 28 Euros
g. five liters of gasoline

ATIVIDADE 40·2

Listen to two people being served at a gasoline station. Write in the table what they require and how much.

	QUANTITY OF GASOLINE				QUANTITY OF OIL
normal	4-star	unleaded	diesel		
1. _____	_____	_____	_____	_____	
2. _____	_____	_____	_____	_____	

Take part in a conversation at a gasoline station, following the prompts below.

1. Good morning. Please fill up the tank.

2. Normal, unleaded, please.

3. Do you have oil?

4. Two liters.

5. Do you sell maps of the region?

6. OK. Thank you. Goodbye.

Língua

To say *nearest, furthest, fastest, cheapest,* etc. you use **mais** (*more*) and the relevant adjective (**próximo, longe, rápido, barato,** respectively):

mais próximo	*nearest*
mais longe	*furthest*
mais rápido	*fastest*
mais barato	*cheapest*

If you are describing an object, such as *the fastest train*, the word order is: **o comboio mais rápido** (*the train more fast*). Remember also to make the adjectives agree in gender (masculine/feminine) and number (singular/plural):

a camisa mais barata	*the cheapest blouse*
as praias mais próximas	*the nearest beaches*

De interesse

Um posto de gasolina (*a small gasoline station*) will usually only have a couple of gasoline pumps, and not many are open 24 hours. On country roads you may only come across **uma bomba de gasolina** (*a single gasoline pump*), which is open for even fewer hours. If you need help with your vehicle on the road, you will need to find **uma estação de serviço** (*a service station,* most of which are 24-hour businesses now, with all vehicle facilities and a shop), or, in the towns, **uma oficina de reparos/automóveis** (*a car-repair garage*). Gasoline in Portugal is now **gasolina sem chumbo** (*unleaded*) for most normal cars.

In Brazil you can get **gasolina** or **combustível, álcool** (*ethanol*) and **gás** (*liquefied petroleum gas*), but unleaded is not available everywhere.

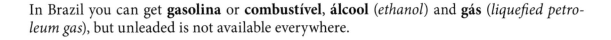

Directions

Traveling by car

VOCABULÁRIO

ajuda [f.]	*help*
caminho [m.]	*way*
chegará	*you will arrive*
complicado	*complicated*
devagar	*slow(ly)*
diz	*(it) says*
dizer	*to say*
é só	*you only have to, it's just . . .*
estrada [f.]	*road*
Pare!	*Stop!* (command)
parece	*it seems*
passagem de peões/passadeira [f.];	*pedestrian crossing*
[BP] a passagem para pedestres	
rotunda [f.]	*roundabout*
seguir	*to follow*
semáforos [m., pl.];	*traffic lights*
[BP] o sinal (luminoso)	
sinais de trânsito [m., pl.]	*road signs*
sinal [m.]	*sign*
voltar para trás	*to turn back*

🔘 Diálogo

VISITOR: O senhor desculpe, pode me dizer se este é o caminho para Loulé?

MAN: Para Loulé? Não é por aqui. A senhora tem que voltar para trás até aos semáforos. Depois, precisa de virar à direita e tomar a estrada para Vila Real. Logo vai ver uma rotunda—é só seguir o sinal que diz Loulé, e pronto, chegará.

VISITOR: Parece um pouco complicado. É longe?

MAN: Não é muito longe. Loulé fica a uns trinta e cinco quilómetros daqui.

VISITOR: Está bem. Obrigada pela ajuda.

Match the road signs to the captions.

1.    a. Passadeira

2.    b. Semáforos

3.    c. Siga em frente

4.   d. Proibido virar à direita

5.    e. Cuidado—animais

Listen to someone asking for road directions and write down where the speaker is going; whether he/she is on the right track; the direction at the traffic lights; and how far the final destination is.

_____

_____

_____

Now take part in a dialogue, where you will be asked for road directions. Follow the prompts below.

1. For Viseu? It's not through here.

2. Turn back to the traffic lights, and then turn left and take the road for Guarda.

3. Next you will see a roundabout—just follow the sign for Viseu, and there you are.

4. Yes, it is a bit far. Viseu is some 95 km from here.

Língua

There are two ways of saying *for* in Portuguese: **por** and **para**. They also have various other meanings and usages:

por	*for/through/by/along*
para	*for/direction to/towards*

As you saw in Unit 17, remember that **por** becomes **pelo**, **pela**, **pelos**, **pelas** when contracted with the words for *the*.

o caminho **para** Loulé	*the way to Loulé*
Vamos passar **pelo** parque.	*Let's go through the park.*

You will come across further usages of **por** and **para** as you learn more Portuguese.

De interesse

Driving in Portugal can be very hit and miss (sometimes, unfortunately, quite literally!). Roads are often in a bad state of repair and drivers seem oblivious to the laws and etiquette of driving. Some stretches of road are notoriously dangerous, such as the coastal stretch between Lisbon and Estoril, known as the **Marginal**, which is considered one of the most dangerous in Europe.

It's not much better in Brazil, so you take your life in your hands if you venture out in a vehicle in larger cities. Drivers hurtle at great speed, often with scant regard for traffic lights or other recognizable rules of the road.

Town amenities

Sports and leisure facilities

VOCABULÁRIO

adultos [m., pl.]	*adults*
além de	*as well as/besides*
além disto	*as well as this*
andar a cavalo	*to ride a horse*
campo de golfe [m.]	*golf course*
centro de lazer [m.]	*leisure center*
centro hípico [m.]	*horse riding center*
clube [m.]	*(sports) club*
correr	*to run*
crianças [f., pl.]	*children*
de barquinho	*by (small) boat*
desportos [m., pl.];	*sports*
[BP] **os esportes**	
fazer piquenique	*to have a picnic*
futebol [m.]	*football*
jogar	*to play (sports/games)*
lago [m.]	*lake*
municipal	*municipal/public*
parque [m.]	*park*
passeio [m.]	*walk/ride/stroll*
piscina [f.]	*swimming pool*
sócio [m.]	*member*
ténis [m.]; [BP] **o tênis**	*tennis*

🔘 Diálogo

AO TURISMO *(at the tourist office)*

WOMAN: Bom dia. Diga, se faz favor.

VISITOR: Bom dia. Queria saber se tem informações sobre os desportos na cidade.

WOMAN: Claro. Nesta cidade temos uma boa piscina municipal, que abre todos os dias menos segunda. Também há um clube de futebol e outro de ténis.

VISITOR: E para a família?

WOMAN: Bom, além da piscina, há dois parques onde uma família pode fazer piquenique, correr, e fazer um passeio de barquinho no lago.

VISITOR: Há um campo de golfe?

WOMAN: Aqui não há, mas há um bom clube na cidade mais próxima, só que tem que ser sócio para jogar. Além disto, há um centro hípico onde pode andar a cavalo, na estrada de Lagoa.

ATIVIDADE 42·1

Fill in the blanks in the text with the following words:

hípico   ténis   piquenique   piscina   campo   jogar   desportos   cavalo   sócio   parque

Aqui pode fazer muitos _____. Na cidade há uma _____ e um centro _____ onde pode andar a _____. Também há um bom _____ de golfe e um clube de _____ mas tem que ser _____ para _____. Uma família pode fazer _____ no _____.

ATIVIDADE 42·2

Listen to someone inquiring about leisure facilities and check off what is available.

horse riding   _____

park   _____

golf course   _____

football   _____

tennis club   _____

picnic areas   _____

swimming   _____

boating lake   _____

Imagine you want to find out about certain leisure facilities and go to the **turismo** *to ask about availability and opening times.*

1. Good morning. Do you have any information on the sports in the city?

2. Does the swimming pool open every day?

3. Do you have to be a member to play golf?

4. Where is the golf course?

5. Thank you.

Língua

The Portuguese like to add—**inho/a** to the end of words. This has the effect of not only making an object seem smaller, for example, **um barco** (*boat*) → **barquinho** (*little boat*), but can also make words and phrases sound friendlier, cuter, and more expressive:

obrigado/a	*thank you*	→ **obrigadinho/a**	*thanks*
um pouco	*a little*	→ **um pouquinho**	*a tiny bit*
um prato	*a plate/dish*	→ **um pratinho**	*small plate/'nibbles'*

De interesse

Portugal does not have an extensive system of **centros de lazer** (*leisure centers*), even in the larger cities. Most places at least have **uma piscina municipal** (*public swimming pool*), where most young people descend en masse during the summer. Brazilians and Portuguese also prefer to spend leisure time on the beach if they can, so **ténis**, **futebol**, and **vôlei** are popular activities. Middle-class Brazilians may belong to a private **clube** where they often spend weekends by the pool or on the tennis courts.

Downtown
Shopping for souvenirs

VOCABULÁRIO

à mão	*by hand*
à procura de	*looking for, on the look-out for*
artesanato [m.]	*crafts*
azulejos [m., pl.]	*ornamental tiles*
bordadas [f., pl.]	*embroidered*
brincos [m., pl.]	*earrings*
compra	*you (he/she) buy*
cores [f., pl.]	*colors*
desde . . . até . . .	*from . . . (up) to . . .*
embrulhar	*to wrap up*
fábrica [f.]	*factory*
filigrana [f.]	*filigree work*
galo de Barcelos [m.]	*Barcelos cockerel* (typical symbol of Portugal)
nacional	*national*
painéis [m., pl.]	*tile panels*
pesado	*heavy*
por exemplo	*for example*
preto	*black*
recomenda	*(you) recommend*
símbolo [m.]	*symbol*
típica [f.]	*typical*
toalhas de mesa [f., pl.]	*tablecloths*
tudo	*everything*
uma lembrança	*a souvenir*
vermelho	*red*
xaile [m.]	*a shawl*

🔘 Diálogo

CUSTOMER: Bom dia, minha senhora. Estou à procura duma lembrança típica de Portugal para a minha mulher. O que recomenda?

ASSISTANT: Tenho umas coisas muito lindas para senhoras. Por exemplo, há estas toalhas de mesa brancas, bordadas à mão. Também há em vermelho.

CUSTOMER: Tem azulejos?

ASSISTANT: Tenho sim. Aqui estão. Há desde estes pequenos até estes grandes painéis.

CUSTOMER: Não quero nada muito pesado.

ASSISTANT: Então, por que não compra um galo de Barcelos, que é o nosso símbolo nacional? As cores são bonitas—laranja, vermelho, azul e preto.

CUSTOMER: Boa ideia. Também vou levar este xaile e estes brincos de filigrana. Pode me embrulhar tudo?

ASSISTANT: Claro.

ATIVIDADE 43·1

Put the correct form of the adjective in these sentences. Remember to check if the objects are masculine or feminine, and singular or plural.

1. Quero um xaile _____ (preto), por favor.

2. Temos estas toalhas de mesa _____ (vermelho).

3. Vou levar estes brincos _____ (lindo).

4. Os painéis são muito _____ (pesado).

5. Por que não leva um galo _____ (nacional).

ATIVIDADE 43·2

Listen to a conversation in a gift shop and mark the appropriate columns in the table what there is to buy.

GIFT	YES	NO	RED	WHITE	BLACK	ORANGE	BLUE	NO SPECIFIC COLOR
Barcelos cockerel	____	____	____	____	____	____	____	____
tablecloths	____	____	____	____	____	____	____	____
tiles	____	____	____	____	____	____	____	____
tile panels	____	____	____	____	____	____	____	____
shawl	____	____	____	____	____	____	____	____

Now take part in a dialogue in a gift shop, where you are looking for souvenirs.

1. Good morning. I'm looking for a typical souvenir of Portugal for my daughter. What do you recommend?

2. Do you have any black shawls?

3. Do you have any tiles?

4. I don't want anything very heavy.

5. Good idea, and I'll also take a black shawl.

Língua

Tudo is a neutral word which means *all* or *everything* when nothing specific is referred to. It never changes form, unlike the adjective **todo** (**toda**, **todos**, **todas**), meaning *all the* or *every*, which agrees with the words it is describing:

todos os dias	*every day* (lit. *all the days*)
toda a maça	*all the apple*

But:

Quero **tudo**.	*I want everything.*
É **tudo** muito bonito.	*It's all really beautiful.*

De interesse

Lembranças (*souvenirs*) are many and varied in Portugal and Brazil. **Artesanato** (*crafts*) are widespread, and in country areas you can often see people creating their products—weaving, making pottery, lace, etc. **Cerâmica** (*earthenware pottery*) is popular in the North of Portugal, and cheaper in the smaller towns. **Renda** (*lace*) often comes in from Madeira and is a little more pricey, but exquisite and well worth the price. **Azulejos** (*tiles*) are available everywhere—you can buy number tiles for your house at a very low price, up to full size picture panels, which are much more expensive. In Lisbon search out the factory which makes them, the Fábrica de Sant'ana. Brazilian crafts include exquisite handmade articles in natural materials (wood, feathers, leather), often produced by the indigenous people.

Personal choices

Talking about sports and hobbies

VOCABULÁRIO	
a cabeça	*the head*
a mente	*the mind*
a óleo	*in oils*
andar de bicicleta	*to go bike riding*
detesto	*I detest*
faz bem	*(it) is good/does good*
faz mal	*(it) is bad/does bad*
fumar	*to smoke*
jornais [m., pl.]	*newspapers*
ler	*to read*
mesmo	*even*
música [f.]	*music*
nadar	*to swim*
odeia	*hate(s)*
ouvir	*to hear, listen to*
praticar (desportos); [BP] esportes	*to play (sports)*
prefere	*prefer(s)*
preferido; *also* favorito/predileto	*favorite*
romances policiais [m., pl.]	*police novels*
tempo de lazer [m.]	*leisure time*
tempo livre [m.]	*free time*

 **Diálogo**

PEDRO: O que é que tu gostas de fazer no tempo livre?

ANA: Gosto muito de praticar desportos sempre que posso.

PEDRO: E qual é o teu desporto preferido?

ANA: Adoro nadar, e também jogar golfe.

PEDRO: Não gostas de fazer coisas em casa?

ANA: Em geral detesto ficar em casa, mas de vez em quando gosto de pintar a óleo. E tu, Pedro, o que é que fazes no teu tempo de lazer?

Pedro: Eu prefiro ficar em casa a ouvir música e a ler. Adoro passar umas horas a ler jornais e romances policiais. A minha mulher odeia ficar dentro de casa—ela prefere andar de bicicleta, mesmo no inverno!

Ana: Faz bem à saúde.

Pedro: Sim, mas o ler faz bem à mente!

ATIVIDADE 44·1

The verbs underlined are all in the wrong position! Put them in the correct sentence and give the correct meaning to the text.

Gosto muito de ir à piscina para <u>andar</u>. A minha filha prefere <u>pintar</u> jornais em casa, e o meu filho adora <u>ouvir música</u> a óleo. Pessoalmente, detesto <u>nadar</u> de bicicleta, mas gosto de <u>ler</u> jazz.

_____

_____

_____

ATIVIDADE 44·2

Listen to the following survey about what two people do in their free time and write down in the space provided what each person does/doesn't like doing.

Speaker 1 likes _____

does not like _____

Speaker 2 likes _____

does not like _____

Imagine you are Senhora Silva and you are being asked about your hobbies. Follow the prompts below and respond to the interview on the recording.

1. I like riding a bike and swimming.

2. The bike.

3. I sometimes like listening to music.

4. My husband likes reading. He hates sports.

Língua

In English we often use verbs to convey the meaning of an action-noun, as in reading, smoking, walking, etc. In Portuguese you can convey these forms by using the structure **o** + verb in the infinitive (its normal form):

O ler faz bem à mente	*Reading is good for the mind.*
O fumar faz mal.	*Smoking does harm.*
O andar é bom.	*Walking is good.*

De interesse

The Portuguese are very keen on music, from country-style folk groups (**ranchos folclóricos**) who sing and dance, to the national **fado**, which can either be sombre and nostalgic, or livelier and evocative. They also like opera, jazz, classical and modern rock. The *Portuguese guitar* (**a guitarra portuguesa**), heard in **fado**, is unlike the Spanish: it is pear-shaped, has double metal strings, and is a surviving relation of the zither.

Brazilian music has long entertained the world, and few people have not heard its catchy rhythms, as it has travelled well on the world music scene. The "greats" of Brazilian music include Caetano Veloso, Chico Buarque, Gal Costa, Milton Nascimento, among many, many more. Brazilian music covers a wide range of styles, and you would be hard-pressed not to find something to your own taste.

Vacations

Discussing last year's holidays

VOCABULÁRIO	
adorámos; [BP] adoramos	we loved
cansativo	tiring
cheios [m., pl.] de	full of
emoção [f.]	excitement
foi	it was
fomos	we went
gostámos; [BP] gostamos (no accent)	we liked
gostaram	you (pl.) (they) liked
gostei	I liked
México [m.]	Mexico
o ano passado [m.]	last year
passei	I spent time
passou	you (he/she/it) spent
perdemos	we lost
positiva [f.]	positive
uma experiência	an experience
viagem [f.]	journey
vimos	we saw
visitámos; [BP] visitamos	we visited
visitei	I visited

Diálogo

JÚLIA: Onde passou as últimas férias?

JOÃO: O ano passado eu e a minha mulher fomos para os Estado Unidos.

JÚLIA: E gostaram?

JOÃO: Gostámos, mas perdemos uma mala e eu não gostei muito da comida.

JÚLIA: Mas foi uma experiência positiva?

JOÃO: Foi, sim. Vimos muitas coisas novas, visitámos muitas cidades e praias e fomos até ao México.

JÚLIA: Foi cansativo?

JOÃO: Um pouco, sim, mas adorámos a viagem, e chegámos ao hotel cheios de emoção.

Choose the correct verb to fill in the blanks in these sentences.

a. BEBEMOS   b. PERDEMOS   c. VISITÁMOS   d. VIMOS   e. CHEGÁMOS   f. ADORÁMOS

1. A semana passada _____ Dallas.

2. _____ a comida.

3. _____ muito vinho.

4. Nas férias _____ muitas coisas novas.

5. _____ às dez horas.

6. Infelizmente, _____ as nossas malas.

Listen to three speakers describe their holidays last year, and fill in the missing information in the table below.

	WENT TO	WITH WHOM	LIKED	DIDN'T LIKE	VISITED
1.	_____	_____	_____	_____	_____
2.	_____	_____	_____	_____	_____
3.	_____	_____	_____	_____	_____

Take part in a conversation about vacations, using the prompts below to guide you.

1. Last year, I went to Madeira with my family.

2. We liked it a lot, but my wife did not like the food.

3. Yes, we visited Funchal and saw the 'levadas'.

4. Yes, but it was also a little tiring.

Língua

In Unit 36 you were introduced to the past tense of some verbs. Here is a table of some other verbs in the past tense you may want to use at this stage.

		eu	tu	ele/ela/você o senhor/ a senhora	nós	eles/elas/vocês os senhores/ as senhoras
beber	*drink*	bebi	bebeste	bebeu	bebemos	beberam
comer	*eat*	comi	comeste	comeu	comemos	comeram
chegar	*arrive*	cheguei	chegaste	chegou	chegámos	chegaram
gostar	*like*	gostei	gostaste	gostou	gostámos	gostaram
visitar	*visit*	visitei	visitaste	visitou	visitámos	visitaram
ver	*see*	vi	viste	viu	vimos	viram
ir	*go*	fui	foste	foi	fomos	foram

This past tense in Portuguese translates both as *I have done* and *I did/I drank/I have drunk,* etc.

| **Comi** muito. | *I have eaten a lot/I ate a lot.* |
| Ela **visitou** a França. | *She has visited France/She visited France.* |

The verb **ir** has the same verb forms in this tense as **ser** (*to be*), as in the dialogue **foi cansativo** (*it was tiring*). You need to look and listen logically to the context to check which verb makes most sense: **foi uma experiência positiva**—*it went* or *it was a positive experience*?

De interesse

There are almost one and a half million Portuguese people currently living in the United States, many working in the hotel and catering industry, and approximately one million Brazilians.

The weather

Talking about climates

VOCABULÁRIO

chove	*it rains*
demasiado	*too (much)*
Grã-Bretanha [f.]	*Great Britain*
igual	*the same, equal*
mais ou menos	*more or less*
Não aguento . . .	*I can't stand . . . , I hate . . .*
não sabia	*I didn't know*
parecido	*alike, same*
perfeito	*perfect*
refrescante	*refreshing*
seco	*dry*
tão bom	*so good*
tropical	*tropical*
variável	*changeable*

Diálogo

CHARLES: Eu gosto imenso de Portugal porque o clima é tão bom.

ALEXANDRA: Nem sempre, Charles. No inverno o clima cá é bastante variável. No sul é quente, e, às vezes, também chove; no centro e no norte é frio.

CHARLES: Ah, sim? Eu não sabia. Então, o clima do inverno é parecido com o nosso, na Grã Bretanha. Mas o clima da primavera e do verão é melhor, não é?

ALEXANDRA: Sim, é. O nosso clima de verão em geral é quente e seco; do norte a sul, e do oeste ao leste, é mais ou menos igual.

CHARLES: Não aguento um clima demasiado frio, nem tropical. Portanto, Portugal é perfeito para mim.

ATIVIDADE
46·1

*Look at the dialogue below, then say whether these statements are **verdadeiro** or **falso**.*

1. No inverno, o clima em Portugal é variável. _____

2. No sul, é muito frio no inverno. _____

3. O clima em Portugal no inverno é diferente do clima da Grã-Bretanha. _____

4. O clima de verão em Portugal não é muito quente. _____

5. O Charles não gosta do clima frio. _____

ATIVIDADE
46·2

Listen to a description of the varying climate in different parts of Brazil and write in the table the details you are given.

	NORTH	SOUTH	EAST	WEST
summer	_____	_____	_____	_____
winter	_____	_____	_____	_____

ATIVIDADE
46·3

Now take part in a dialogue about the climate in Great Britain. Follow the prompts below.

1. Not always, Maria. Our climate here is quite variable.

2. In the winter it is cold in the north and it rains a lot.

3. In the summer it is hot in the south and quite hot in the north.

4. It is a little, but the climate in Portugal in the spring and summer is better.

5. I don't like too hot a climate, so the climate in Great Britain is perfect for me.

Língua

Don't forget that when talking about climates you will use the verb **ser**, the "permanent" *to be* verb, because climates are a fixed characteristic of an area. However, if you are talking about the weather on a particular day you should use *estar*:

O clima em Portugal **é** muito bom.	*The climate in Portugal is very good.*
O tempo hoje não **está** bom.	*The weather today isn't good.*

De interesse

Current climatic changes around the globe have also affected parts of Portugal. Long, dry periods and, at the other extreme, heavy rainfalls, both continue to bring chaos to the country at different times in the year.

Brazil, too, has suffered extensive problems due to rainfall in recent years, particularly in Rio and São Paulo, where horrendous landslides wiped out many of the **favela** (*slum*) dwellings on the sides of the cities.

Ill health

A trip to the hospital

VOCABULÁRIO	
(fui) atropelado/a	*(I was) knocked down*
atravessar	*to cross*
chapéu [m.]	*hat*
gesso [m.]	*plaster cast*
inchado	*swollen*
joelho [m.]	*knee*
lavar	*to wash*
mandar	*to send*
médico [m.]	*doctor*
O que aconteceu?	*What happened/has happened?*
partido; *also* **quebrado**	*broken*
penso (que)	*I think (that)*
pulso [m.]	*wrist*
radiografia [f.]; *also* **um raio-X**	*X-ray*
sentar-se	*to sit down*
tentei	*I tried*
tirar	*to take*
torcido	*twisted, sprained*
tornozelo [m.]	*ankle*
um momentinho	*just a short time, (for) just a moment*

Diálogos

WOMAN: Faz favor, preciso ver um médico.

RECEPTIONIST: Qual é o problema?

WOMAN: Penso que tenho o pulso partido, e doem-me o tornozelo e o joelho.

RECEPTIONIST: Um momento, sim? Quer sentar-se um momentinho?

DOCTOR: O que aconteceu?

WOMAN: Tentei atravessar a avenida hoje de manhã, e fui atropelada por uma bicicleta.

DOCTOR: Vou mandar a senhora tirar uma radiografia. O pulso está partido. Vai ter que ficar quatro semanas em gesso. Também a senhora tem um tornozelo torcido, e o joelho está inchado. Vai ter que descansar muito.

Fill in the blanks in these sentences with the following words. Use each word once.

um   um   uma   um   inchado   partido   médico   tornozelo   gesso   pulso   radiografia

1. Vou ter que ficar três semanas com um gesso porque tenho _____.

2. Faz favor, preciso de ver _____.

3. O joelho está partido, então vai ter que ficar em _____.

4. A senhora precisa de tirar _____ porque tem um pulso partido.

5. Vai ter que descansar a mão muito porque tem _____.

Listen to two patients being told what is wrong with them, and what the remedy is, and write in the table below. You may need to review Unit 35 for parts of the body.

	AFFECTED LIMB	PROBLEM	PLASTER CAST?	HOW LONG?	REST?	HOW LONG?
1.	_____	_____	_____	_____	_____	_____
2.	_____	_____	_____	_____	_____	_____

Now imagine you have had an accident and you need to visit the hospital. Start the dialogue with the first prompt below.

1. I need to see a doctor, please.

2. I think I have a broken ankle.

3. This morning a bicycle knocked me down.

4. Am I going to have to rest?

Língua

When talking about parts of the body, you do not need to use the words for *my, your,* etc. You simply refer to the part of the body, unless you need to emphasise whose body is affected:

Tenho **o pulso** partido.	*My wrist is broken. (lit. I have the wrist broken.)*
Vai lavar **as mãos**.	*Go and wash your hands. (lit. Wash the hands.)*
Ele tem **o dedo** inchado, mas **o meu dedo** está bem.	*He has a swollen finger, but my finger is OK.*

This also applies to clothing:

Vou pôr **o chapéu**.	*I'm going to put my hat on.*
	(lit. I'm going to put on the hat.)

In Portuguese, certain verbs, like the verb *to sit down,* **sentar-se**, are followed by a pronoun (**se**) which means *self* (**sit oneself down**). These are called reflexive verbs, and they are used with these reflexive pronouns:

-me	*me, myself*
-te	*you (fam.), yourself*
-se	*himself/herself/itself/yourself (polite)*
-nos	*us, ourselves*
-se	*themselves/yourselves (pl.)*

In English, the word *self* is not always present (as in *sit down*). As with other pronouns, the reflexive goes before the verb in negatives and questions, otherwise its normal place is after, unless you are in Brazil, where it is usually always found before the verb: **ele se sentou** (*he sat down*).

De interesse

Modern **centros de saúde** (*health centers*) in Portugal are very efficient and accessible to foreign visitors who produce passport ID. Larger cities in Brazil have good health provisions, but at a price! However, most pharmacists in Brazil can treat most minor ailments efficiently, so your first port of call can be the **farmácia**.

Time

Asking the time

VOCABULÁRIO	
à hora	*on time*
a tempo	*in time*
acabas de . . .	*you (fam.) have just . . .*
achar	*to find*
apressar-se	*to hurry*
Calma!	*Calm down!*
carro [m.]; *also* automóvel	*car*
começa	*(it) begins*
começar	*to begin*
divertir-nos	*to enjoy ourselves*
estacionar	*to park*
estamos	*we are*
Faltam . . . minutos.	*There are . . . minutes (before).*
mesmo à hora	*right on time*
peça [f.]	*play*
perguntar	*to ask (a question)*
Que horas são?	*What time is it?*
são . . .	*it is . . . (lit. they are)*

Diálogo

CARLOS: Que horas são, Paula?

PAULA: São sete e um quarto.

CARLOS: Bom, ainda chegamos a tempo.

PAULA: A que horas começa a peça?

CARLOS: Às oito. Que horas são agora?

PAULA: Acabas de perguntar—agora são sete e vinte.

CARLOS: Faltam quarenta minutos para começar a peça, e ainda temos que achar um lugar onde estacionar o carro, comprar os bilhetes, e sentar-nos. Temos que nos apressar. Que horas são, Paula?

PAULA: São oito menos dez. Calma, Carlos. Aqui estamos. Chegámos mesmo à hora. Vamos divertir-nos.

Match each of these watches and clocks with the correct time. **Que horas são?**

1.

2.

3.

4.

5.

a. cinco e meia

b. sete horas

c. dez menos um quarto

d. nove e vinte

e. quatro menos dez

f. nove menos quarenta e cinco

g. seis horas.

Listen to three short conversations where people ask the time, and say what time a shop is due to open or close. Fill in the information below.

	WHAT TIME IS IT?	GOING WHERE?	OPEN AT?	CLOSED AT?
1.				
2.				
3.				

Imagine you are trying to get to the bank on time. Take part in a dialogue like the one on the previous page.

1. Sandra, what time is it?

2. Good, we'll still arrive in time.

3. At three.

4. Yes, but we still have to find a place to park the car.

5. We've arrived right on time. Let's go in.

Língua

Asking and giving the time is very similar to what you learned in Unit 24. The question **Que horas são?**, will be answered with **São . . .**, except when it is one o'clock, midday and midnight, when the time will be preceded by **é . . .**, eg. **é meia-noite** (*it is midnight*). You can also ask someone the time by asking **Tem as horas?**, and say **faltam (X) minutos para as (Y) (horas)**, for example, instead of **são oito menos dez**, **faltam dez para as oito** (*it's ten to eight*).

De interesse

The Portuguese and Brazilians are not usually exacting when it comes to time-keeping. Don't be surprised to be kept waiting if you arrange to meet people, and, if you are invited to a Portuguese or Brazilian home for a social event, it's quite acceptable not to keep to a **hora pontual**.

People

Talking about age

┌─── VOCABULÁRIO ───┐

avó [f.]	*grandmother*
avô [m.]	*grandfather*
avós [m., pl.]	*grandparents*
conhecer	*to meet/get to know*
dia de anos [m.]; [BP] and *also* [EP]: o aniversário	*birthday*
faço...anos; [BP] meu aniversário é...	*I have a birthday*
faleceu	*he/she passed away*
fazer anos	*to have a birthday*
fez...anos	*was...years old*
neta [f.]	*granddaughter*
neto [m.]	*grandson*
netos [m., pl.]	*grandchildren; also grandsons*
o mais velho [m.]	*the oldest*
o/a mais...	*the most...*
Quantos anos têm?	*How old are they?*
tia [f.]	*aunt*
tio [m.]	*uncle*
tios [m., pl.]	*uncles and aunts*

Diálogo

ANTÓNIO: Anne, venha conhecer os meus netos. Este é o meu neto Mário, e esta é a minha neta Luísa.

ANNE: Muito prazer. Quantos anos têm?

ANTÓNIO: O Mário, que é o mais velho, tem dez anos, e a Luísa, que é mais nova, tem oito.

ANNE: Eles são muito bonitos.

ANTÓNIO: Ainda tem os avós, Anne?

ANNE: Tenho duas avós, e um avô, mas o outro faleceu. Mas tenho muitos tios. A minha tia Mary fez setenta anos a semana passada.

ANTÓNIO: E quando é o seu dia de anos, Anne?

ANNE: Faço anos no dia quinze de setembro.

Match the descriptions to the birthday cards below.

1. A avó de Sônia fez sessenta e cinco anos.

a.

2. O avô de Roberto fez oitenta anos.

b.

3. O Fernando tem vinte e um anos.

c.

4. A minha neta Alice vai fazer quinze anos.

d.

5. A Marli fez dezoito anos.

e.

Listen to three people from José's family saying what their relation to him is and what their ages are. Fill in their details in the table.

	RELATION TO JOSÉ	AGE
1.	_____	_____
2.	_____	_____
3.	_____	_____

Now take part in a conversation about family members and their ages. Follow the prompts below.

1. Paulo, come and meet my children.

2. David, who is the oldest, is sixteen and Laura, who is younger, is fourteen.

3. David's birthday is on the twenty-fifth of March and Laura had her birthday last week.

4. My birthday is on the third of November.

Língua

When talking about ages, you use the verb **ter** (*to have*), plus the number of **anos** (*years*) someone has. You will need to know the relevant forms of the verb:

eu	tu	ele/ela/*you*	nós	eles/elas/*you* (pl.)
tenho	tens	tem	temos	têm

To have a birthday is fazer anos (lit. *to make years*), so you may need forms of the verb **fazer**:

eu	tu	ele/ela/*you*	nós	ele/elas/*you* (pl.)
faço	fazes	faz	fazemos	fazem

Note how the date is done: **no dia dez de junho** (*on the tenth of June*). Note also how to make comparisons:

mais velho/a	*older*
o/a mais velho/a	*the oldest*
mais novo/a	*younger*
o/a mais novo/a	*the youngest*

De interesse

The Portuguese and Brazilians enjoy birthday parties, and big family gatherings often take place when an older member of the family is celebrating. A huge spread is usually laid out, with lots of extremely tempting sweets!

Eating out

Making a complaint

VOCABULÁRIO	
acontecem	*(they) happen*
cerveja [f.]	*beer*
colher [f.]	*spoon*
conta [f.]	*bill*
copo [m.]	*glass*
de volta; *also* **devolver** (*to return something*)	*back*
demora [f.]	*delay*
enfim	*after all*
errado	*wrong*
faca [f.]	*knife*
falta/faltam	*is/are missing, lacking*
garfo [m.]	*fork*
mandámos; [BP] **mandamos**	*we sent*
morno	*warm*
movimentado	*busy*
não pedimos	*we did not order/have not ordered*
peço desculpa	*I'm sorry*
pela demora	*for the delay*
peru [m.]	*turkey*
rachado	*chipped, scratched*
sujo	*dirty*
trazer	*to bring*
umas coisinhas	*some little things*

Diálogo

CUSTOMER: Faz favor!

WAITER: Diga, faz favor.

CUSTOMER: Faltam dois garfos e uma faca aqui, e esta colher está suja. Pode trazer outros?

WAITER: Com certeza. Um momento só.

WAITER: Pronto, aqui estão. Peço desculpa pela demora—hoje está muito movimentado, e, enfim, estas coisas acontecem.

CUSTOMER: Só mais umas coisinhas—o bacalhau está frio, a cerveja está morna, o copo está rachado e a salada não está boa.

CUSTOMER: Faz favor. Acho que a conta está errada. Nós não pedimos o peru, e mandámos a salada de volta.

WAITER: Vou verificar.

ATIVIDADE 50·1

Match the Portuguese and English expressions. There are two extra English ones.

1. A colher está suja.

2. O copo está rachado.

3. Falta uma faca.

4. A conta está errada.

5. O peru está frio.

a. There's a knife missing.

b. The spoon is dirty.

c. There's a fork missing.

d. The bill is wrong.

e. The glass is chipped.

f. The cup is dirty.

g. The turkey is cold.

ATIVIDADE 50·2

Listen to three people making complaints and write the columns what the problem is.

	ITEM	PROBLEM
1.	_____	_____
2.	_____	_____
3.	_____	_____

Imagine you are eating out and you have some problems you need to complain about. Let the prompts guide you through a conversation with the waiter.

1. Excuse me!

2. There are two knives missing and this fork is dirty. Can you bring some others?

3. Another thing, the turkey isn't good, and this glass is chipped.

Língua

To say something is missing, or lacking, use **falta** for one item and **faltam** for more than one. You can use these verbs as follows:

Falta dinheiro.	*There's no money/not enough money.*
Falta tempo.	*There's no time/not enough time.*
Faltam dez minutos para as três.	*It's ten to three. (lit. There are ten minutes lacking to the three.)*

De interesse

The Portuguese word for *turkey* has an interesting historical origin. When Spanish and Portuguese explorers arrived in Peru, they found a strange bird which was a local delicacy, and highly venerated. It was brought back to the Iberian Peninsula and in Portugal was named after the land whence it came—**o peru**.

Accommodations

When things don't work

VOCABULÁRIO	
a noite inteira	*the whole night*
abafado	*stuffy*
alguém	*somebody*
apartamento [m.]	*apartment*
ar condicionado [m.]	*air-conditioning*
chuveiro [m.]	*shower*
dar uma olhadela; [BP] uma olhada	*to have a look*
descongelar	*to defrost*
em primeiro lugar	*firstly*
frigorífico [m.]; [BP] a geladeira/	*refrigerator*
o refrigerador	
inteiro	*entire, whole*
lavatório [m.]	*washbasin*
não funciona	*(it) doesn't work*
ninguém	*nobody*
pingar	*to drip*
por conseguinte	*consequently*
Quais são . . . ?	*What/which are . . . ?*
torneira [f.]	*tap*
totalmente	*totally*

Diálogo

GUEST: Estamos no apartamento vinte e três, e temos alguns problemas.

RECEPTIONIST: Quais são os problemas?

GUEST: Bom, em primeiro lugar, o chuveiro não funciona-não há água quente. Também a torneira no lavatório não fecha totalmente, e a água está a pingar a noite inteira.

RECEPTIONIST: Vou ver se alguém pode ir dar uma olhadela para os senhores.

GUEST: Há outra coisa, parece que o ar condicionado não funciona bem, e por conseguinte está muito abafado dentro do quarto. O frigorífico não está muito frio, e a comida começou a descongelar.

RECEPTIONIST: Vou ver se há outro apartamento.

GUEST: Boa ideia!

ATIVIDADE 51·1

Fill in the gaps in these sentences with suitable words from the list below.

água   comida   fecha   frigorífico   chuveiro   condicionado

1. O _____ não está frio.

2. O ar _____ não funciona bem.

3. Não há _____quente.

4. A torneira não _____ totalmente.

5. O _____ não funciona.

6. A _____ está a descongelar.

ATIVIDADE 51·2

Listen to two people making complaints about their apartments, and mark the appropriate column below with which problems each one has.

	1	2
shower not working	_____	_____
tap won't turn off	_____	_____
air-conditioning not working	_____	_____
fridge not working	_____	_____

*Using the **Língua** section below as a guide, answer negatively the questions on the recording.*

Example:

Tem alguma laranja?   *Do you have an orange?*
Não tenho nenhuma.   *I don't have one (any).*

Remember to use the correct form of the verb **ter** in each case.

Língua

Ways of expressing *some* and *none*: these agree (match endings) with the item they refer to.

Masculine Singular		Feminine Singular		Masculine Plural		Feminine Plural	
algum	*a*	**alguma**	*a*	**alguns**	*some*	**algumas**	*some*
nenhum	*a/one (none)*	**nenhuma**	*a/one (none)*	**nenhuns**	*any/none*	**nenhumas**	*any/none*

Maria tem **algumas** blusas.   *Maria has some blouses.*
Não tenho **nenhum** jornal.   *I don't have a/any newspaper.*

You can also express *a/some* simply by using the appropriate words you learned in Units 3 and 7 (**um/uma/uns/umas**):

Tenho **umas** amigas muito bonitas   *I have some very pretty friends.*

Alguém (*somebody/someone/anyone*) and **ninguém** (*nobody/no one*) never change form.

Alguém tem dinheiro?   *Does anyone have (any) money?*
Ninguém está aqui.   *Nobody is here.*

De interesse

Problems with water and drainage are probably the most common for vacationers in Portugal. In the Algarve, there may be water restrictions from time to time. The drainage system is poor in many places, and it is commonplace not to flush paper down the toilet, but to dispose of it in the wastepaper baskets provided!

Travel

Air travel

VOCABULÁRIO

a declarar	*to declare*
aeroporto [m.]	*aiport*
alfândega [f.]	*customs*
balança [f.]	*weighing scales*
chegada [f.]	*arrival*
controlador [m.] de bagagem	*luggage check-in attendant*
nada	*nothing*
oficial [m.] da alfândega	*customs official*
passageiro [m.]	*passenger*
porta [f.]	*gate (door)*
saco [m.]	*bag, carrier bag*
saída [f.]	*exit/departure*
um atraso	*a delay*
voo [m.]	*flight*

🔊 Diálogos

DEPARTING

ATTENDANT: O senhor tem passaporte e bilhete?

PASSENGER: Sim, aqui.

ATTENDANT: Quer passar a sua mala à balança se faz favor?
Só tem esta?

PASSENGER: Só, e este saco que vou levar comigo.

ATTENDANT: Está bem. O voo BA 123 para Londres vai ter um
atraso de uma hora. Pode passar para a porta número dezoito.

ARRIVING

CUSTOMS OFFICIAL: Tem alguma coisa a declarar?

PASSENGER: Não tenho nada.

OFFICIAL: O senhor quer abrir a mala, se faz favor?

Fill in the blanks in this dialogue at the airport.

CONTROLADORA: O senhor tem _____ e bilhete?

PASSAGEIRO: Sim, _____ (here).

CONTROLADORA: _____ (will you) passar as suas

         _____ (suitcases) à balança, se faz favor? (Only)

         _____ tem estas?

PASSAGEIRO: Só (and) _____ este saco que (I'm going)

         _____ levar comigo.

CONTROLADORA: (OK) _____ O voo BA 287 para

         _____ (Italy) vai ter um atraso de

         _____ (35 minutes). Pode passar para a

         (gate) _____ número _____ (fifteen).

Listen to the announcement of three flights in the airport and mark in the table the missing information.

FLIGHT NO.	DESTINATION	DELAY?	HOW LONG?	GATE NO.
1. _____	_____	_____	_____	_____
2. _____	_____	_____	_____	_____
3. _____	_____	_____	_____	_____

You are going to be the check-in attendant, dealing with a passenger. Let the prompts below guide you.

1. Do you have passport and ticket, sir?

2. Do you want to pass your suitcase onto the scales?

3. Do you only have this one?

4. Flight TAP 567 to Faro is going to have a delay of twenty minutes.

5. You can pass to gate number 14.

Língua

Quer (*do you want, would you like*), is also used to mean *would you mind . . .*, as you saw in the dialogue:

Quer passar a sua mala?	*Would you mind passing (over) your suitcase?*
O senhor **quer** abrir a mala?	*Would you mind opening the suitcase?*

De interesse

Lisbon is a rapidly-evolving city, whose international airport has recently undergone a huge overhaul and expansion to increase its capacity to deal with growing business and tourist visitors to this increasingly-popular cosmopolitan capital.

The main airports you may fly to in Brazil are: Galeão in Rio, Guarulhos in São Paulo, and in the northern regions, Salvador, Recife, Fortaleza and Manaus.

Directions

Getting around the airport

VOCABULÁRIO	
alugar	*to rent, hire*
aluguer [m.]; [BP] o aluguel	*hire, rental*
ao chegar	*on arriving*
automóvel [m.]	*car*
carrinho [m.]	*trolley*
carrossel [m.]; *also* a recolha de bagagens	*baggage reclaim/carrousel*
em frente	*in front, opposite*
em segundo lugar	*secondly*
lavabos [m., pl.]; [BP] o banheiro	*toilets, restrooms*
pergunta [f.]	*question*
Podia . . . ?	*Could you . . . ?*
por ali	*over there*

🔘 Diálogo

TOURIST: Faz favor. Podia me dizer onde são os lavabos no aeroporto?

WOMAN: Claro. O senhor passa por ali, em frente, vira à direita, e vai ver os lavabos mesmo em frente.

TOURIST: Muito obrigado. Agora, mais duas perguntas. Primeiro, preciso de alugar um automóvel e, em segundo lugar, preciso dum carrinho para trazer as malas do carrossel.

WOMAN: Bom, há várias companhias de carros de aluguer por ali, e, depois, há carrinhos para bagagem perto da alfândega. É só virar aqui à esquerda e ao chegar à alfândega vai ver os carrinhos ao lado.

TOURIST: Obrigado.

WOMAN: De nada.

ATIVIDADE 53·1

Fill in the spaces in these sentences with a verb from list A, or an item from list B. Each sentence practices the verb **precisar de** (to need), *which you learned about in Unit 11.*

A	B
fazer	carrinho
pagar	vinho
comprar	dinheiro

1. Preciso de _____ um jornal.

2. Tu precisas de _____ para beber.

3. O João precisa dum _____ .

4. Nós precisamos de _____ a conta.

5. Os senhores precisam de _____ as compras.

6. Eles precisam de _____ .

ATIVIDADE 53·2

Listen to two people asking for information at the airport, and mark down what they are looking for, and which direction it is.

LOOKING FOR WHAT?   WHERE IS IT?

1. _____   _____

2. _____   _____

ATIVIDADE 53·3

Imagine you are the information clerk at the airport. Two people will ask you for help. Use the prompts below to guide you through the dialogue.

1. Of course. You pass down there, straight ahead, turn left, and you will see the car hire, right in front.

2. Of course. You just turn right here and, when you arrive at customs, you will see the toilets on the left.

3. Don't mention it.

Língua

Ao chegar means *on arriving/on arrival/when you arrive.* This is quite a common structure in Portuguese, and is easy to form: **ao** + verb in the infinitive:

ao pagar a conta. . .	*on paying the bill . . .*
ao sair da casa . . .	*on leaving the house . . .*
ao visitar o museu . . .	*on visiting the museum . . .*

Podia (or **poderia**), meaning *could you,* like **queria** and **gostava,** which you met in Unit 32, is an example of a conditional in Portuguese. In English we use *could* and *would,* especially in polite requests, as in the dialogue.

In the example **podia me dizer . . .** the **me** is another pronoun, this time being the object of the verb. Object pronouns can either be direct, answering the questions *What?* or *Whom?,* or indirect, answering the question *To/for what or whom?* In our example *me* is indirect—*Can you tell (it) to me?*

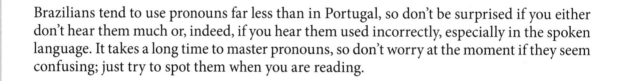

	I	*you (fam.)*	*he/she/it/you*	*we*	*they/you (pl.)*
direct	me	**te**	**o/a**	**nos**	**os/as**
indirect	me	**te**	**lhe**	**nos**	**lhes**

Brazilians tend to use pronouns far less than in Portugal, so don't be surprised if you either don't hear them much or, indeed, if you hear them used incorrectly, especially in the spoken language. It takes a long time to master pronouns, so don't worry at the moment if they seem confusing; just try to spot them when you are reading.

De interesse

All major towns have at least two or three main car-hire firms operating in them. If you intend to drive in Portugal, make sure you have a licence, insurance, and permission to drive the vehicle, if it is not actually yours. Otherwise spot-traffic checks can be an ordeal.

Brazilian traffic police are also notoriously difficult to deal with. You will need your own driving licence in Brazil, but may also avoid problems with authorities if you also carry an International Drivers Permit, available from national motoring associations.

Town amenities

Buying bus tickets at the kiosk

VOCABULÁRIO

ao entrar	*when you enter/get on (on entering)*
avenida [f.]	*avenue*
elétricos [m., pl.]	*trams*
elevador [m.]; *also* **o ascensor**	*lift*
forma [f.]	*form, type*
funiculares [m., pl.]	*funicular railcars*
metro [m.]; [BP] o metrô	*subway, underground*
módulo [m.]	*type of ticket (see* De interesse*)*
motorista [m.]	*driver*
paga	*you (he/she/it) pay(s)*
poupa	*you (he/she/it) save*
transporte [m.]	*transportation*
vale a pena	*it's worth it*
vale	*(it) is worth*

Diálogo

TOURIST: Bom dia, senhor. Queria saber quanto custa um bilhete de autocarro até à Avenida do Brasil.

ATTENDANT: Bom, se não tem módulos, paga ao motorista ao entrar.

TOURIST: Que são módulos?

ATTENDANT: Pode-se comprar aqui, cada módulo vale duas viagens aqui no centro. Assim a senhora poupa dinheiro.

TOURIST: E pode-se usar no metro também?

ATTENDANT: No metro não, mas pode-se usar nos funiculares, nos elétricos e no Elevador de Santa Justa na Baixa.

TOURIST: Que boa ideia! Já que vou estar aqui algumas semanas, vale a pena.

ATIVIDADE 54·1

*Jane has a book of **módulos** to use on transportation. Write out in full in Portuguese how much she would spend if she made the following journeys in the centre, if each **módulo** costs 1 Euro and 20 cents, and each can be used for two journeys.*

1. two journeys _____

2. five journeys _____

3. one stop only _____

4. seven journeys _____

5. three journeys _____

ATIVIDADE 54·2

*Re-read and listen again to the **diálogo** and choose the correct answers to these questions.*

1. What does the tourist want to know?
   a. how much a bus ticket is
   b. where the Avenida do Brasil is

2. Can you use the módulos on the subway?
   a. no
   b. yes

3. How long is the tourist going to be in Lisbon?
   a. a few days
   b. a few weeks

ATIVIDADE 54·3

Now take part in a dialogue at a ticket kiosk. Supply your part of the dialogue below. The correct version for your lines is on the recording and in the answer key.

1. (say) Good morning. How much is a bus ticket to the Baixa?

   Se não tem módulos, a viagem custa 70 cêntimos.

2. (say) Can one use them on the trams?

   Sim, pode-se usar em todas as formas de transporte menos no metro.

3. (say) In that case, I would like six, please.

Língua

Pode-se is an impersonal way of saying *you can*. You take the third (he/she) part of the verb and add **se**. It actually means *one can/people can/it is possible* and if you have studied French, it is equivalent to the **on** form. It is used when the information given is relevant to everyone in general and not just the person addressed. Other similar examples you may come across include:

Precisa-se dum médico.	*A doctor is needed.*
Fala-se inglês.	*English (is) spoken.*

In Brazil you are more likely to find the **se** before the verb, so se pode, se fala, etc., or even not at all!

De interesse

Buying **módulos** is an excellent way of saving money if you intend being in a Portuguese town for any length of time. You can also buy a **passe** of varying lengths and types. The **Cartão Lisboa Viva** is also a discount card for travel and cheap entry to various locations of interest.

Brazilian buses are very cheap, and widely used by commuters, schoolchildren, and everyone going about their daily lives. Just hop on, pay the fare, and off you go!

The **Elevador de Santa Justa** is a marvellous lift designed by Eiffel. It takes people up from the lower part of Lisbon, known as the Baixa, to the upper part, Bairro Alto.

Downtown

Buying groceries

VOCABULÁRIO	
açúcar [m.]	*sugar*
Assim dá.	*That'll do.*
Chega!	*Enough!*
chouriço [m.]	*spicy sausage*
diga lá	*say then, say what you want*
farinha [f.]	*flour*
manteiga [f.]	*butter*
meia dúzia [f.]	*half a dozen*
presunto [m.]	*smoked ham* (ordinary ham in Brazil)
provar	*to try, taste*
Que é isto?	*What is this?*
queijo fresco [m.]	*cottage cheese*
sem sal	*without salt*
um garrafão	*a demijohn, large bottle*
um pacote	*a packet*
uma caixinha	*a small box/tub*

Diálogo

SRA BROWN: Boa tarde, senhor Pereira. Preciso dumas coisas.

SR PEREIRA: Então, diga lá. O que quer?

SRA BROWN: Quero meio quilo de açúcar, um pacote de manteiga sem sal, e um quilo de farinha.

SR PEREIRA: Vai fazer um bolo?

SRA BROWN: Vou, sim. O meu neto faz anos no domingo.

SR PEREIRA: Precisa de mais aluguma coisa?

SRA BROWN: Sim. Também quero cinco fatias de presunto, uma caixinha de queijo fresco e, o que é isto aqui?

SR PEREIRA: É chouriço novo da serra (*from the mountain*).

SRA BROWN: Então, vou levar um pouco para provar. Trezentos gramas, se faz favor. Chega! Assim dá.

SR PEREIRA: Que mais?

SRA BROWN: Meia dúzia de ovos e um garrafão de água.

SR PEREIRA: Mais?

SRA BROWN: É tudo. Obrigada.

Fill in the blanks with the following words.

garrafão   queijo   sal   quilo   pouco   ovos

Quero meio _____ de farinha, uma dúzia de _____ , um _____ de água, manteiga sem _____ e um _____ de _____ fresco.

Here is Ana's **lista de compras** *(shopping list). As she goes through her list on the recording, check off everything she asks for. You will find one item is overlooked. Which one?*

a dozen eggs
half kilo butter
two tubs of cottage cheese
demijohn of water
three slices of smoked ham
200 g spicy sausage
kilo of flour
packet of sugar

Now take part in a dialogue at the grocer's following the prompts on the recording to guide you.

1. Good morning, Mr Silva. I need some things.

2. I want a kilo of flour and 300g of spicy sausage.

3. Yes, I also want half a kilo of sugar.

4. A dozen eggs and a packet of butter.

5. That's all. Thanks.

Língua

It is quite acceptable, with people who are not complete strangers, to use **quero** (*I want*) instead of **queria** (*I would like*). It is not considered impolite, and its use is widespread among Portuguese and Brazilian native speakers.

De interesse

Chouriço is a very popular, spicy, continental-style sausage, found in various Portuguese meals, including the delicious shredded kale soup **caldo verde**. Other spicy sausage words include **linguiça** (also used in Brazil), and the black/blood puddings **farinheira** and **mortadela**.

Personal choices

Favorite modes of transportation

VOCABULÁRIO	
(ir) ao estrangeiro	*(to go) abroad*
... demais	*too ...*
Apanho; [BP] pego	*I catch*
barato	*cheap*
Como vais para ...?	*How do you (fam.) get to ...?*
confortável	*comfortable*
dá-me; [BP] me dá	*(it) gives me*
de avião	*by plane*
de moto	*by motorbike*
de táxi	*by taxi*
eficiente	*efficient*
fico enjoado	*I get sick*
hora de ponta [f.]	*rush hour*
lento	*slow*
rápido	*fast*
saudável	*healthy*
Tenho medo.	*I'm afraid.*

Diálogo

PEDRO: Ana, gostas de viajar de avião?

ANA: Adoro. É muito rápido, confortável e eficiente. Quando vou
ao estrangeiro sempre vou de avião.

PEDRO: Não preferes ir de barco?

ANA: Não. Acho o barco demasiado lento, e sempre fico enjoada.
Acho um pouco caro também.

PEDRO: Também não gosto tanto de barcos. Como vais para o
trabalho? Vais de carro?

ANA: Às vezes. Mas a hora de ponta dá-me dor de cabeça, então
às vezes apanho o autocarro, ou vou a pé.

PEDRO: Ir a pé é muito saudável e barato, mas lento demais para
mim. Quando tenho pressa vou de táxi. Aos fins de semana
gosto de passear de moto.

ANA: As motos vão muito rápido para mim. Tenho medo de
viajar assim. Prefiro andar a cavalo.

Match up the pictures both to one of the following descriptive words as well as to the labels to the right.

rápido   barato   caro   lento   eficiente   confortável

1. _____   a. de barco

2. _____   b. de carro

3. _____   c. de táxi

4. _____   d. de moto

5. _____   e. de avião

Listen to two people say what their favorite and least favorite means of transportation are and why. Fill in the table below.

FAVORITE	REASON	LEAST FAVORITE	REASON
1. _____	_____	_____	_____
2. _____	_____	_____	_____

Now take part in a discussion on the recording about transportation.

1. I love it. It's comfortable and cheap.

2. No, I think the plane is too expensive for me.

3. Sometimes I go by bus, or sometimes on foot.

4. I don't like traveling by motorbike—it's too fast for me.

Língua

Modes of transportation are conveyed by **de** + transport, except for **a pé** (*on foot*) and **a cavalo** (*on horseback*).

> **Demasiado** and **demais** both mean *too*. **Demasiado** is placed before the adjective, and **demais** after:
>
> | | |
> |---|---|
> | Esta blusa é **demasiado** cara. | *This blouse is too expensive.* |
> | Esta blusa é cara **demais.** | |
>
> Often people just use the word **muito** (*very*):
>
> | | |
> |---|---|
> | Esta blusa é **muito** cara para mim. | *This blouse is very/too expensive for me.* |

De interesse

Traveling around in Portugal has become easier, as new highway infrastructures now link the major cities on main routes, and comfortable express trains (including the modern Alfa Pendular) run between Oporto, Lisbon and the Algarve. In Brazil, long-distance travel is still the domain of the bus, or done by car or plane.

Vacations

·57·

Talking about a cultural holiday/vacation

VOCABULÁRIO

Acabo de voltar.	*I've just returned.*
achei	*I found, thought*
antigo	*old*
arte [f.]	*art*
casas [f., pl.] de fado	*fado (music) houses*
catedrais	*cathedrals*
catedral [f.] *also* **a Sé**	*cathedral*
culturais	*cultural [pl.]*
cultural	*cultural*
havia	*there was/there were*
houve	*there was/were, has been/have been*
interessante	*interesting*
magnífico	*magnificent*
o Jardim Botânico	*the botanical garden*
realmente	*really*
século [m.]	*century*
tantas coisas [f., pl.]	*so many things*
um panorama	*a panoramic view*
uma exposição	*an exhibition*
voltou	*you've (he/she/it's) returned*

🔘 Diálogo

JÚLIA: Olá, João. Então, já voltou das férias?

JOÃO: Sim, acabo de voltar. Foi uma semana ótima.

JÚLIA: O que fez?

JOÃO: Fui a Lisboa e passei a semana a fazer coisas culturais.

JÚLIA: Foi ao Museu Gulbenkian?

JOÃO: Fui, sim. Havia uma exposição de pinturas do século dezoito, que achei muito interessante. Também visitei o Museu de Arte Antiga.

JÚLIA: Foi ao Castelo de São Jorge?

JOÃO: Só passei uma hora lá—não houve tempo para fazer tudo. Gostei muito do castelo—havia um panorama magnífico da cidade.

JÚLIA: Lisboa é uma cidade realmente bonita.

JOÃO: Há tantas coisas para fazer—as Casas de Fado, as catedrais e palácios, o Jardim Botânico, o teatro. Na verdade, precisa—se dum mês para ver tudo.

ATIVIDADE 57·1

Fill in the spaces with the correct past form of the verbs in parentheses. You may need to review Unit 45.

1. Eu (ir) _____ ao castelo.

2. O José (passar) _____ uma semana em Lisboa.

3. Eles (visitar) _____ o museu.

4. Tu (gostar) _____ do Jardim Botânico?

5. A senhora (ver) _____ uma exposição.

ATIVIDADE 57·2

Listen to three people talking about the places they have visited, when they visited, and how much time they spent there. Make a note in the table below.

	WHERE?	WHEN?	HOW LONG?
1.	_____	_____	_____
2.	_____	_____	_____
3.	_____	_____	_____

ATIVIDADE 57·3

Take part in a dialogue about some cultural activities you have participated in.

1. I went to London and spent the week doing cultural things.

2. Yes, I did (go). There was an exhibition of paintings from the sixteenth century.

3. I only spent two hours there. There wasn't time to do everything.

4. Yes, there are so many things to do.

Língua

Havia and **houve** both mean *there was* and *there were* and are the equivalents of **há** in the past. **Houve** is often used in time expressions and for one-off actions, and **havia** in giving descriptions.

The dialogue contains more examples of words ending in **-l**, which form their plural in **-is**: **cultural/culturais**; **catedral/catedrais**. Both nouns and adjectives work in this way. Try to learn these as you go along, and be aware that irregularities also occur.

When talking about centuries, ordinal numbers (1ˢᵗ, 2ⁿᵈ, etc.) are used up to ten (**primeiro, segundo, terceiro, quarto, quinto, sexto, sétimo, oitavo, nono, décimo**) and cardinal numbers (11, 12, 13, etc.) thereafter (**século: onze, treze, etc.**).

De interesse

The **Casas de Fado** are where you will hear typical Portuguese fado music. They are mostly found in Lisbon, Oporto and Coimbra, and are often restaurants. When the singer, flanked by her (or his) two guitarists, is ready to sing, the lights will be dimmed, and it is etiquette to listen in silence. If the singer is particularly good, on the penultimate line of the song, which rises to a crescendo, it is practice to shout out **Ó, fadista** in recognition of their skill.

The weather

Talking about yesterday's weather

VOCABULÁRIO	
baixou	*(it) went down*
chovia/estava a chover; [BP] estava chovendo	*it was raining*
espalhava-se; [BP] se espalhava	*was spreading/scattering*
esteve	*it (he/she/you) was (were)*
eu tive	*I had*
feio	*bad/ugly*
geada [f.]	*frost*
gelar	*to freeze*
horrível	*awful*
lixo [m.]	*rubbish*
não pude	*I couldn't, I was not able*
nevar	*to snow*
quem me dera	*if only I could . . .*
relâmpagos [m., pl.]	*lightning*
tanto . . . que	*so much . . . that*
tempestade [f.]	*storm*
trovoadas [f., pl.]	*thunder*

🔘 Diálogo

MIGUEL: Que dia feio esteve ontem! Não pude sair.

LÚMEN: Eu sei. Foi horrível. De manhã chovia e depois começou a nevar também.

MIGUEL: Depois do almoço havia muito vento e o lixo espalhava-se todo pela rua.

LÚMEN: O tempo começou a ficar muito mau—com trovoadas e relâmpagos. Eu tive muito medo.

MIGUEL: Era uma verdadeira tempestade. À noite a temperatura baixou, e começou a gelar. Creio que hoje vamos ter geada.

LÚMEN: Quem me dera viver num país quente!

ATIVIDADE
58·1

Match the pictures to the captions.

1.

a. geada

2.

b. relâmpagos

3.

c. chovia

4.

d. trovoadas

5.

e. neve

ATIVIDADE
58·2

You will hear two people saying what kind of weather there was on certain days. Fill in the table with the relevant information.

DAY   WEATHER

1. _____   _____

2. _____   _____

Take part in a dialogue about yesterday's weather.

1. I know. I couldn't get out. It was very windy.

2. I think we'll have frost today.

3. If only I could live in a tropical country!

Língua

Often when talking about past weather, we look at what was happening throughout certain periods of time, and in Portuguese we use a past tense of the verb, known as the imperfect, which is different to the one you have already been introduced to.

Imperfect	Continuous Meaning
Havia vento, neve.	*There was wind, snow.*
Chovia or **estava** a chover. (BP **estava** chovendo)	*It was raining.*

Compare these examples with the past tense you have already learned (known as the preterite):

Ontem **choveu**.	*Yesterday it rained.*
Esteve muito frio.	*It was very cold.*

This tense describes a fixed, single action, or confined space of time, and not a continuous, on-going one as in the imperfect.

De interesse

In the winter, the region of Serra da Estrela in Portugal, situated in the center-east of the country and towards the Spanish border, is covered in snow, and has its own winter ski resort.

In the south of Brazil, although snow is pretty rare, the Gaucho regions of Rio Grande do Sul, Santa Catarina, and Paraná get temperatures as low as 50° F (10° C) in the winter months from June to August.

Ill health

Dealing with an accident

VOCABULÁRIO

acidente [m.]	*accident*
ajudar	*to help*
ambulância [f.]	*ambulance*
bombeiros [m., pl.]	*fire service, firefighters*
chocaram	(they) *bumped* (into each other)
exatamente	*exactly*
feridas [f., pl.]	*injured*
houve	*there has been*
ligaduras [f., pl.]; [BP] bandagens	*bandages*
pensos [m., pl.]; [BP] band-aids	*plasters, band-aids*
ponto de referência [m.]	*reference point*
precisamos	*we need*
serviços [m., pl.] de emergência	*emergency services*
Venha depressa!	*Hurry up!*

Diálogo

WOMAN: Serviços de emergência. Diga o que quer.

MAN: Houve um acidente. Precisamos duma ambulância.

WOMAN: Onde aconteceu o acidente?

MAN: Estamos na esquina da Rua Camões com a Rua da Sé.

WOMAN: E qual é o problema exatamente?

MAN: Dois carros chocaram um com o outro. Há três pessoas feridas. Temos um médico aqui a ajudar com ligaduras e pensos, mas isto é uma emergência.

WOMAN: Precisam dos bombeiros também?

MAN: Não sei, provavelmente.

WOMAN: Qual é o seu nome, por favor?

MAN: Chamo-me Roberto dos Santos. Trabalho perto daqui na farmácia.

WOMAN: E qual é o ponto de referência mais próximo?

MAN: É o Banco Sol, na Rua Camões. Estamos bem perto. Venha depressa, por favor.

Read the dialogue again, and mark in the columns below whether these statements are **verdadeiro** or **falso**.

	V	F
1. Precisa-se duma ambulância.	___	___
2. O acidente aconteceu na Rua do Sol.	___	___
3. Três carros chocaram-se.	___	___
4. Há pessoas feridas.	___	___
5. O Sr dos Santos trabalha no banco.	___	___

Listen to someone giving details of an accident and fill in the table below.

WHERE IS ACCIDENT?	HOW MANY INJURED?	NAME OF CALLER	POINT OF REFERENCE
_____	_____	_____	_____

Now imagine you have to contact the emergency services about an accident. Follow the prompts below.

1. There's been an accident. We need an ambulance.

2. On the corner of Sé Street and Brazil Street. There are five people injured.

3. (Give your own name.)

4. The Mendes Chemist. Hurry up, please!

Língua

The word **problema**, although ending in **-a** is actually masculine. There are a number of words which do not conform to the normal rules of gender, such as **o chá** (*tea*) **o telegrama** (*telegram*), and **o cinema** (*cinema*). Keep an eye out for them as you go along in your learning.

Venha depressa! (*Hurry up!*) is an example of a polite command as you learned in Unit 29. Other irregular commands you may come across include:

fazer	*to do/make*
Faça!	*Do/make!*
ver	*to see*
Veja!	*See!*
pôr	*to put*
Ponha!	*Put!*

You have also seen **traga** (*bring*) and **dê** (*give*).

De interesse

The emergency phone number in Portugal is 112, and it is a free number. In Brazil, you need 190 for the police, 192 for an ambulance, and 193 for the fire service. Talking on the phone in any other language is always difficult, so explain you are foreign, and ask the operator to speak slowly. Try to give as much information about the accident as possible, including the nearest reference points.

Time

Departure and arrival times

VOCABULÁRIO	
à espera de	waiting for
Aceita...?	Will you accept...?
Aceito...	I accept...
Até à próxima!	See you next time!
atrasado	late/delayed
Boa viagem!	Bon voyage!
check-in [m.]	check-in
chegarão	you [pl.] (they) will arrive
chegaremos	we shall arrive
Com muito gosto!	With much pleasure!
Espero que tenha gostado...	I hope you (have) enjoyed...
Não tenho certeza.	I'm not certain/sure.
Obrigada por tudo.	Thanks for everything.
partirá	it (he/she/you) will depart
partiremos	we shall depart
sala de espera [f.]	waiting room
um dia destes	one of these days
visita [f.]	visit
voltarei	I shall return

Diálogos

ANTÓNIO: Então, Anne, a que horas vai partir?

ANNE: Não tenho a certeza, António. Creio que está atrasado. Espere aqui um momento, vou perguntar.

ANNE: Por favor, estou à espera do voo BA 335 para a Inglaterra. Sabe a que horas partiremos?

ATTENDANT: Este voo partirá às vinte e quinze. Houve um atraso de quarenta minutos por causa do vento.

ANNE: E a que horas chegaremos lá?

ATTENDANT: Provavelmente chegarão às vinte a duas e trinta. Já fez o check-in?

ANNE: Já.

ATTENDANT: Então, pode passar para a sala de espera.

ANTÓNIO: Espero que a Anne tenha gostado da visita a Portugal. Aceita uma pequena lembrança do nosso país?

ANNE: Aceito, sim, com muito gosto . . . Ah! um galo de
Barcelos-o símbolo de Portugal. Muito obrigada. Gostei
imenso de cá estar.

ANTÓNIO: Boa viagem, e até à próxima!

ANNE: Adeus, e obrigada por tudo. Voltarei um dia destes . . .

ATIVIDADE 60·1

Fill in the blanks in these sentences.

1. O _____ partirá às _____ (10:15)

2. O _____ chegará às _____ (21:20)

3. O _____ chegará às _____ (03:40)

4. O _____ partirá às _____ (08:13)

5. O _____ partirá às _____ (17:50)

ATIVIDADE 60·2

Listen to two people asking about departure/arrive times when traveling. Write down any delay and the reasons for it.

TRANSPORTATION	DEPARTURE	DELAY?	HOW LONG?	WHY?	ARRIVAL
1. _____	_____	_____	_____	_____	_____
2. _____	_____	_____	_____	_____	_____

You are now going to be a ticket clerk at a port. Follow the prompts below.

1. The next boat to Brazil will leave at 10:20.

2. There has been a delay of two hours because of the bad weather.

3. The boat will probably arrive at 8:30 A.M. on Thursday.

4. Have you checked in yet?

5. Well then, you can pass to the waiting room.

Língua

The future tense, although often replaced by the more colloquial use of the verb **ir**, *to go* (*I'm going to . . .*), is, nevertheless, handy to know. The formation is the same for all verbs. The following endings are simply added to the verb infinitive:

eu	tu	ele/ela/você/you	nós	eles/elas/vocês/you pl
+EI	+ÁS	+Á	+EMOS	+ÃO
chegarei	chegarás	chegará	chegaremos	chegarão
entrarei	entrarás	entrará	entraremos	entrarão
partirei	partirás	partirá	partiremos	partirão

There are just three exceptions—**fazer** (*to do*), **trazer** (*to bring*), **dizer** (*to say*). Their forms are:

farei	farás	fará	faremos	farão
trarei	trarás	trará	traremos	trarão
direi	dirás	dirá	diremos	dirão

De interesse

The Portuguese Barcelos cockerel is a symbol of peace and harmony. Legend has it that an innocent man was condemned to die, until a roasted cockerel stood up and crowed to prove his innocence. From that day forwards, the cockerel has been used to symbolize the spirit of these very generous people

Portugal, Madeira, and the Azores are great destinations for short, or long-term visits. The people will extend a warm welcome to visitors, both old and young alike, and now that you can speak some Portuguese, you will find a whole new world awaiting you on arrival.

If your destination is further away, in Brazil, or even one of the former Portuguese colonies in Africa, such as Angola, you will definitely make use of your new-found Portuguese. And with the pending Olympic Games and World Cup to visit Brazil, there is no better time to get hold of this language and get out there!

Grammar summary

Nouns

All things, objects, people, and abstract ideas are nouns. In Portuguese, all nouns are either masculine or feminine, and are divided into masculine and feminine groups which may, or may not, have a logic to the novice language learner.

	Masc. sing.	Fem. sing.	Masc. pl.	Fem pl.
Regular *o/a* endings	o barco	a casa	os livros	as mesas
Irregulars	o papel	a estação	os jornais	as nuvens

Articles

These are the words for *the* (definite article) and *a/an, some* (indefinite article) that go in front of a noun, and they depend on whether the noun they go with is masculine or feminine.

	Masc. sing.	Fem. sing.	Masc. pl.	Fem. pl.
Definite (*the*)	o	a	os	as
Indefinite (*a, an*)	um	uma	uns (some)	umas

Subject pronouns

These are the words for those who are carrying out the action of the verbs.

eu	*I*
tu	*you (fam.)*
ele	*he (it)*
ela	*she (it)*
você/o senhor/a senhora	*you*
nós	*we*
eles (m.)	*they*
elas (f.)	*they*
vocês/os srs/as sras	*you (pl.)*

Verbs

In dictionaries, verbs are always listed in their infinitive (the *to* form of the verb). Portuguese infinitives fall into three groups according to their endings: for example, **falar** (*to speak*), **comer** (*to eat*), **partir** (*to leave*). There are also many irregular verbs that do not follow these patterns.

Regular verbs

These are the tenses you have been introduced to during this course.

- **Present:** I speak, do speak, etc.

	eu	tu	ela/ela/você	nós	eles/elas/vocês
-ar	falo	falas	fala	falamos	falam
-er	como	comes	come	comemos	comem
-ir	parto	partes	parte	partimos	partem

- **Preterite:** I spoke, have spoken, etc.

	eu	tu	ela/ela/você	nós	eles/elas/vocês
-ar	falei	falaste	falou	falámos	falaram
-er	comi	comeste	comeu	comemos	comeram
-ir	parti	partiste	partiu	partimos	partiram

- **Imperfect:** I was speaking, used to speak, etc.

	eu	tu	ela/ela/você	nós	eles/elas/vocês
-ar	falava	falavas	falava	falávamos	falavam
-er	comia	comias	comia	comíamos	comiam
-ir	partia	partias	partia	partíamos	partiam

- **Future:** I shall speak, etc.

	eu	tu	ela/ela/você	nós	eles/elas/vocês
-ar	falarei	falarás	falará	falaremos	falarão
-er	comerei	comerás	comerá	comeremos	comerão
-ir	partirei	partirás	partirá	partiremos	partirão

- **Conditional:** I would speak, etc.

	eu	tu	ela/ela/você	nós	eles/elas/vocês
-ar	falaria	falarias	falaria	falaríamos	falariam
-er	comeria	comerias	comeria	comeríamos	comeriam
-ir	partiria	partiria	partiria	partiríamos	partiriam

Irregular verbs

The following verbs all have irregularities in one or more tense. You will find references to them in more extensive grammar books.

dar	*to give*
dizer	*to say*
estar	*to be*
fazer	*to do/make*
ir	*to go*
poder	*to be able*
pôr	*to put*
ser	*to be*
ter	*to have*
ver	*to see*
vir	*to come*

Progressive/continuous tense (...*ing*)

The progressive tense, for example, *to be doing* (at this moment/currently), is formed by adding the following: **estar** + **a** + infinitive.

Estou a falar.	*I am speaking.*

In Brazilian Portuguese, however, it is formed by adding **estar** + gerund. The gerund endings are:

-ar verbs	**-ando**
-er verbs	**-endo**
-ir verbs	**-indo**

Ela **está comendo.**	*She is eating.*

Reflexive verbs

These are joined to a reflexive pronoun (*self*), and are used either to do action to oneself, or in expressions such as ... *is done.* The pronouns are:

me	*myself*
te	*yourself*
se	*his/her/yourself/itself*
nos	*ourselves*
se	*yourselves/themselves*

Lavo-**me.**	*I wash myself.*
Me lavo. [BP]	
Sentam-**se.**	*They sit (themselves) down.*
Se sentam. [BP]	

Ser/Estar/Ficar

Three ways of translating *to be*:

- **Ser** is used for: permanent situations, locations, professions, inherent characteristics.

  sou, es, é, somos, são

- **Estar** is used for: temporary situations, locations, feelings, weather, changeability.

  estou, estás, está, estamos, estão

- **Ficar** is used for: permanent locations, changes of feelings/behavior, to stay.

  fico, ficas, fica, ficamos, ficam

Ela **é** professora.	*She is a teacher.*
O livro **está** debaixo da mesa.	*The book is under the table.*
As lojas **ficam** longe.	*The shops are a long way off.*
O tempo **ficou** frio.	*The weather became cold.*

Commands

Ways of telling people to do something:

	tu	*você (o sr/a sra)*	Plural
-ar verbs	Fala!	Fale!	Falem!
-er verbs	Come!	Coma!	Comam!
-ir verbs	Parte!	Parta!	Partam!

Irregular verbs have irregular command forms.

Eg. Dizer (*to say*)	Diz!	Diga!	Digam!
Vir (*to come*)	Vem!	Venha!	Venham!
Ter (*to have*)	Tem!	Tenha!	Tenham!

Adjectives

Adjectives describe a noun. They agree (match) in number (singular or plural) and gender (masculine or feminine) with the noun they are describing, and are usually placed after the noun. Most follow the regular ending patterns of **o → a**, but many have irregular spellings:

	Masc. sing.	**Fem. sing.**	**Masc. pl.**	**Fem. pl.**
Regular	amarelo	amarela	amarelos	amarelas
Irregular	cultural	cultural	culturais	culturais

a casa **moderna**	*the modern house*
os livros **pretos**	*the black books*

Some adjectives are more likely to appear before the noun, for example, **bom, boa, bons, boas** (*good*): **boa tarde, é um bom filme.**

Demonstratives

Words used for pointing at things or people (*this/that/these/those*):

	Masc. sing.	**Fem. sing.**	**Masc. pl.**	**Fem. pl.**
This/These	este	esta	estes	estas
That/Those	aquele	aquela	aqueles	aquelas

Possessives

Words that show to whom something belongs:

	Masc. sing.	**Fem. sing.**	**Masc. pl.**	**Fem. pl.**
my	o meu	a minha	os meus	as minhas
your (fam.)	o teu	a tua	os teus	as tuas
your (polite)	o seu	a sua	os seus	as suas
our	o nosso	a nossa	os nossos	as nossas
your (pl.)	o vosso	a vossa	os vossos	as vossas
his	o...dele	a...dele	os...dele	as...dele
her	o...dela	a...dela	os...dela	as...dela
their	o...deles/ delas	a...deles/ delas	os...deles/ delas	as...deles/ delas

The possessive agrees with the thing possessed, and not the possessor.

as nossas filhas	*our daughters*
o carro **dela**	*her car* (lit. *the car of her*)

Brazilians tend not to use the articles (**o**, **a**, **os**, **as**) with the possessives.

Prepositions

These are words describing position, place, and time. Here are some of the more common ones:

em	*in, on*
de	*of, about*
por	*for, by*
para	*to, for*
em frente	*in front*
atrás/detrás	*behind*
debaixo	*underneath*
em cima	*on top*
ao lado	*next to*
ao pé	*next to*
a	*to, at*
dentro	*inside*
fora	*outside*
perto	*near*

Many of these can be followed by **de**, for example, **em frente de** (*in front of*) or **em cima de** (*on top of*), and the prepositions **de**, **a**, **em**, **por** combine and contract with definite and indefinite articles, thus:

	o	a	os	as	um	uma	uns	umas
a +	ao	à	aos	às				
de +	do	da	dos	das	dum	duma	duns	dumas
em +	no	na	nos	nas	num	numa	nuns	numas
por +	pelo	pela	pelos	pelas				

ao lado **do** banco	*next to the bank*
Vou **à** igreja.	*I'm going to the church.*
dentro **duma** caixa	*inside a box*

Por and para

Ways of translating *for, to, by*:

	por	**para**
also used for:	price/sending/reason for through/by/along by means of	use/purpose/time for direction towards

por causa da chuva	*because of the rain*
para mim	*for me*

Negatives/interrogatives

Some common negatives and interrogatives (question words) are:

não	*no, not*
nunca	*never*
nada	*nothing*
ninguém	*no one*
nenhum	*none*
nem	*not even*
Onde?	*Where?*
Quando?	*When?*
Como?	*How?*
Porquê?	*Why?*
(o) Quê?	*What?*
Qual?	*Which?*
Quem?	*Who?*

Adverbs

These give more information about how the action of the verb is carried out:

Pode falar **mais devagar**?   *Can you speak more slowly?*

They can also give more description to an adjective:

Ela é **incrivelmente** bonita.   *She is incredibly beautiful.*

Suffixes

These are endings added to certain words to create specific effects. The most common in Portuguese are:

- **-inho (-zinho)** diminutive: makes a word smaller, cuter
- **-ão (zão)** augmentative: makes a word larger, grosser

uma casinha	*a little house*
um garrafão	*a demi-john (large bottle)*

Of course, there is much more to Portuguese grammar than is contained in this course. To progress, you will, at some point, need to purchase a good grammar book, so that you can learn to build up your confidence in constructing your own sentences.

Vocabulary

A

(à) direita *on/to the right*
(à) esquerda *on, to the left*
(ao) lado de *next to*
à mão *by hand*
aberto *open*
abre *(it) opens*
acho (que) *I think (that)*
aconselhável *advisable*
Adeus. *Goodbye.*
adoro *I adore/love*
agora *now*
ainda bem *just as well, thank goodness*
ainda *still, yet*
ajuda [f.] *help*
alemão *German*
alfândega [f.] *customs*
alguém *someone*
alguma coisa [f.] *something*
almoço [m.] *lunch*
alugar *to hire*
amanhã *tomorrow*
amendoeiras [f., pl.] *almond trees*
americano *American*
andar de bicicleta *to ride a bike*
ano [m.] *year*
antes de *before*
antigo *old, antique*
ao pé de *next to*
apartamento [m.] *apartment, flat*
aprender a *to learn to*
aquela [f.] *that, that one*
aqui *here*
às vezes *sometimes*
assim *and so, like this*
assinar *to sign*
até *until, up to, till*
atraso [m.] *delay*
atravessa *you, he, she cross(es)*
atravessar *to cross*
atum [m.] *tuna*
autocarro [m.]; [BP] ônibus *bus*
automóvel [m.] *car*

avenida [f.] *avenue*
azul *blue*
azulejos [m., pl.] *glazed tiles*

B

bacalhau [m.] *(salted) cod*
banco [m.] *bank*
bar [m.] *bar*
barato *cheap*
barco [m.] *boat*
bastante *quite, enough*
batatas [f., pl.] *potatoes*
baunilha [f.] *vanilla*
bem *well*
bem-vinda [f.] *welcome*
biblioteca [f.] *library*
bilhete [m.] *ticket*
bilheteira [f.]; [BP] bilheteria *ticket office*
blusa [f.] *blouse*
Boa ideia. *Good idea.*
Boa noite. *Good evening/night.*
Boa sorte. *Good luck.*
Boa tarde. *Good afternoon.*
Boas férias. *Have a good holiday.*
boate [f.] *nightclub*
bolo [m.] *cake*
bolsa [f.] *bag*
Bom dia. *Good morning.*
bom, boa, bons, boas *good*
bombeiros [m., pl.] *firemen*
bonito *pretty*
braço [m.] *arm*
branco *white*
breve *short, brief*
bronzeador *tanning*

C

cá *here*
cada *each, every*
café [m.] *café, coffee*
calmo *peaceful*
cama [f.] *bed*
caminho [m.] *way, route*

camioneta [f.]; [BP] ônibus *coach*
campo [m.] *countryside*
cansado *tired*
cansativo *tiring*
cão [m.]; [BP] cachorro *dog*
carne [f.] *meat*
caro *expensive*
casa de banho [f.]; [BP] banheiro *bathroom*
casa [f.] *house*
castanha [f.] *chestnut*
castelo [m.] *castle*
cedo *early*
céu [m.] *sky*
chá [m.] *tea*
chamo-me *I am called*
Chega! *Enough!*
chegada [f.] *arrival*
chuva [f.] *rain*
chuveiro [m.] *shower*
cidade [f.] *city, town*
cinema [m.] *cinema*
claro *fair-skinned*
Claro! *Of course!*
Com certeza. *Certainly.*
com *with*
comboio [m.]; [BP] trem *train*
começar *to begin*
começou a *it began to*
comércio [m.] *business*
Como está? *How are you?*
Como se chama? *What is your name?*
comprar *to buy*
confortável *comfortable*
conhecer *to know (person, country)*
conta [f.] *bill*
correr *to run*
costa [f.] *coast*
cozinha [f.] *kitchen/cuisine*
creio *I believe*
creme [m.] *cream, lotion*
crianças [f., pl.] *children*
cuidado *careful*
cuidar de *to take care of*

D

daqui a *from here*
data [f.] *date*
de ida e volta *return (ticket)*
de ida *single (ticket)*
De nada. *Don't mention it.*
De onde é? *Where are you from?*
de urgência *emergency*
de vez em quando *sometimes*
dedo [f.] *finger*
demais *too, too much*
demora [f.] *delay*

dentes [m., pl.] *teeth*
dentro *inside*
depois de *after (doing)*
depois *after, then*
depósito [m.] *petrol tank*
depressa *quickly*
descanso [m.] *rest*
descongelar *to thaw*
Desculpe. *Excuse me.*
detesto *I hate*
detrás de *behind*
devagar *slowly*
deveria *I, you, he, she ought to*
Diga? *Can I help? (lit. say)*
dizer *to say*
dói/doem *hurts/hurt*
dor [f.] *pain*
dose [f.] *helping, portion*

E

e *and*
é *he, she, it is/you are*
elevador [m.] *lift*
em total *in all*
embrulhar *to wrap up*
empada [f.] *pie, pastry*
empresa [f.] *company*
encontrar *to find*
então *well then*
entrada [f.] *entrance/hall*
entre *between*
errado *wrong*
escadas [f., pl.] *stairs, steps*
escola [f.] *school*
esquina [f.] *corner*
está *he, she, it is/you are*
está bem *okay*
esta [f.] *this, this one*
estacionar *to park*
Este é? *Is this?*
este [m.] *this, this one*
estou bem *I'm well*
estou *I am*
estrangeiro [m.] *foreigner/abroad*
estranho *strange*
eu *I*
exatamente *exactly*
excursão [f.] *trip*
experimentar *to try*

F

fábrica [f.] *factory*
fácil *easy*
faço *I do, make*
Fala . . . ? *Do you, does he/she speak . . . ?*
Fala bem. *He/she/you speak(s) well.*

falo *I speak*
falso *false*
farmácia [f.] *pharmacy*
fatia [f.] *slice*
Faz favor. *Please.*
Faz frio. *It's cold.*
fazer as compras [f., pl.] *to do the shopping*
fazer *to do/make*
Fazes? *You do, make?*
fecha *it closes*
fechado *closed*
feio *ugly*
feira [f.] *monthly market, fair*
férias [f., pl.] *holidays*
fiambre [m.]; [BP] presunto *boiled ham*
fica *is situated*
ficar *to be situated*
ficha [f.] *form*
folheto [m.] *leaflet*
fora *outside, out*
fraco *weak*
fresco *fresh, chilled*
fumar *to smoke*

G

galo [m.] *cockerel*
garfo [m.] *fork*
garoto [m.] EP *small, white coffee*
garrafa [f.] *bottle*
garrafão [m.] *demi-john*
gasóleo [m.]; [BP] diesel *diesel*
gasolina [f.] *petrol*
geada [f.] *frost*
gelados [m., pl.]; [BP] sorvetes *ice-cream*
gentil *kind*
geralmente *generally*
gesso [m.] *plaster cast*
ginástica [f.] EP *keep-fit*
gosta de *he, she, you like(s)*
gostaram *they, you (pl) liked*
Gostarias? *You would like?*
Gostas de visitar? *You like to visit?*
Gostei. *I liked.*
Gosto. *I like.*
gramas [m., pl.] *grams*
graus [m., pl.] *degrees*

H

Há quanto tempo? *How much time is there?*
há *there is/are*
havia *there was/there were*
hoje de manhã *this morning*
hoje em dia *nowadays*
hoje *today*
hora de ponta [f.] *rush-hour*
hora [f.] *hour*

horrível *awful*
hotel [m.] *hotel*
houve *there was/were, has been/have been*

I

igreja [f.] *church*
igual *equal, the same*
igualmente *likewise*
imenso *a lot, huge*
inchado *swollen*
incluído *included*
indicativo [m.]; [BP] código *dialing code*
indigestão [f.] *indigestion*
infelizmente *unfortunately*
informações [f., pl.] *information*
informática [f.] *computers, IT*
inteiro *whole*
interessante *interesting*
internacional *international*
inverno [m.] *winter*
ir *to go*
irmã [f.] *sister*
irmão [m.] *brother*
Isto é grave. *This is serious.*

J

Já escolheram? *Have you chosen yet?*
Já está. *There you are.*
já que *given that, as*
já *now, already*
jantamos *we dine*
jantar *to dine*
Jardim Botânico [m.] *botanical garden*
jardim [m.] *garden*
joelho [m.] *knee*
jogar *to play (sport)*
jornais [m., pl.] *newspapers*
junto com *together with*
juntos [pl.] *together*

L

lá *there*
lago [m.] *lake*
laranja [f.] *orange*
lavabos [m., pl.] *toilets, washroom*
lavar *to wash*
lembrança [f.] *souvenir*
lento *slow*
ler *to read*
levar *to take, carry*
lindo *pretty*
linha [f.] *platform*
lista [f.]; [BP] cardápio [m.] *list, menu*
livraria [f.] *bookshop*
livro [m.] *book*
lixo [m.] *rubbish*

logo *then, next*
longe *far*
lugar [m.] *place*

M

Mais alguma coisa? *Anything else?*
mais devagar *more slowly*
mais ou menos *more or less*
mais *more*
mala [f.] *suitcase*
mandar *to send*
manhã [f.] *morning*
manteiga [f.] *butter*
mas *but*
mau tempo [m.] *bad weather*
médico [m.] *doctor*
medida [f.] *size*
meia dose [f.] *half-portion*
meio-dia [m.] *midday*
melhor *better*
menos *less, minus*
mercado [m.] *market*
mercearia [f.] *grocers*
mês [m.] *month*
Mesmo ali. *Right over there.*
minutos [m., pl.] *minutes*
morada [f.] *address*
morango [m.] *strawberry*
morno *warm*
mudança [f.] *change*
muitas vezes *many times, often*
muito bem *very well*
Muito prazer. *Pleased to meet you.*
muito *very, much, a lot*
museu [m.] *museum*

N

nadar *to swim*
Não é? *Isn't it?*
Não seria melhor? *Wouldn't it be?*
não *no, not*
Não, não é. *No, it isn't.*
nas terças *on Tuesdays*
nascimento [m.] *birth*
natural *natural*
negócio(s) [m.] *business*
nem sempre *not always*
nesse caso [m.] *in that case*
nevar *to snow*
neve [f.] *snow*
nome [m.] *name*
normal *normal*
norte [m.] *north*
nota [f.] *note*
novo *young*
nublado *cloudy*
nuvem [f.] *cloud*

O

O que é que? *What is it/that?*
Obrigadinho/a. *Thanks a lot.*
Obrigado/a. *Thank you.*
oeste [m.] *west*
Olá!; [BP] oi! *Hi!*
óleo [m.] *oil*
Onde é que? *Where is it/that?*
Onde fica? *Where is?*
Onde? *Where?*
ora bem *well now*
Ora essa! *Come off it!*
Ótimo! *Great!*
ou *or*
outono [m.] *autumn*
outra coisa [f.] *another thing*
outra vez [f.] *again*
ouvir *to hear*
ovo [m.] *egg*

P

padaria [f.] *baker's*
país [m.] *country*
paisagem [f.] *landscape*
pão [m.] *bread*
para *to, for*
parque [m.] *park*
passageiro [m.] *passenger*
passar *to pass, spend time*
passear *to stroll, wander*
pé [m.] *foot*
pechincha [f.] *bargain*
pequeno *small*
perguntar *to ask*
perigo [m.] *danger*
perto *nearby*
pesado *heavy*
péssimo *awful*
pessoalmente *personally*
pingar *to drip*
piscina [f.] *swimming pool*
pode *you (he, she, it) can*
pois *well*
por *by, for*
porque *because*
Porquê? *Why?*
portanto *therefore*
Posso? *May I?*
pouco *little*
praça [f.] *square*
praia [f.] *beach*
praticar *to practice, play (sports)*
prato [m.] *plate, dish*
precisa-se *is needed*
preencher *to fill in*
preferido *favorite*
primeiro *first*

procurar *to look for*
pronto *ready*
provar *to taste, try*
provavelmente *probably*

Q

Qual é? *What, which is?*
qualidade [f.] *quality*
Quando? *When?*
Quanto é? *How much is it?*
Quantos? *How many?*
quarto [m.] *bedroom*
Quê? *What?*
queijo [m.] *cheese*
quente *hot*
Quer? *Do you want?*
queria *I (you, he, she) would like*
queríamos *we would like*
quintal [m.] *back yard*

R

rachado *chipped*
rápido *fast*
razoável *reasonable*
realmente *really*
receção [f.]; [BP] recepção *reception*
recomendo *I recommend*
reformado; [BP] aposentado *retired*
relâmpago [m.] *lightning*
relaxar *to relax*
remédio [m.] *cure, medicine*
reserva [f.] *reservation*
reservar *to reserve*
rotunda [f.] *circus (road), roundabout*

S

Sabe? *Do you know?*
saber *to know a fact, thing*
sair *to go out*
sapateiro [m.] *shoemender's*
sapato [m.] *shoe*
saudável *healthy*
saúde [f.] *health, cheers (drinking)*
sé [f.] *cathedral*
seco *dry*
seguir *to follow*
sem *without*
semáforos [m., pl.]; [BP] sinais *traffic lights*
sempre *always*
senhor *gentleman, sir*
senhora *lady, madam*
sentar-se *to sit down*

sim *yes*
simpático *nice*
só *only*
sobre *about, over*
sócio [m.] *member*
sol [m.] *sun*
solteiro *single, unmarried*
sou *I am*
subir *to go up*
sujo *dirty*

T

talho [m.]; [BP] açougue *butcher's*
também *also*
tanto *so much*
tarde [f.] *afternoon*
Tem? *Do you have?*
tempo [m.] *weather*
tinto *red (wine)*
típico *typical*
tirar *to take (holidays)*
torneira [f.] *tap*
trabalho [m.] *work*
trânsito [m.] *traffic*
trazer *to bring*
trocar *to change, exchange*
trovoada [f.] *thunder*
tudo *everything*

U

usar *to use*

V

vago *vacant*
vale *it's worth*
Vamos? *Shall we go?*
vários [m., pl.] *several, various*
vento [m.] *wind*
ver *to see*
verdade [f.] *truth*
verdadeiro *true*
verificar *to check*
viagem [f.] *journey*
viajar *to travel*
visitar *to visit*
voltar *to return*
voo [m.] *flight*

X

xaile [m.] *shawl*
xarope [m.] *medicine*

Answer key

1 People: Introductions

1·1   2. Chamo-me Françoise. Sou de Paris.   3. Chamo-me Mark. Sou de Londres.
4. Chamo-me Helga. Sou de Berlim.

1·2   1. Maria/Faro   2. Miguel/Lisboa   3. Eduarda/Lagos

1·3   1. Bom dia. Chamo-me Frank.   2. Sou inglês. Sou de Lancaster.   3. Igualmente.

2 Eating out: Snacks and drinks

2·1   1. uma água mineral   2. um pastel de nata   3. um café e uma empada de galinha

2·2   1. empada/café   2. água mineral/pastel de nata

2·3   1. Queria uma empada de galinha.   2. Sim, queria uma água mineral, se faz favor.
3. Fresca.   4. Com gás.

3 Accommodations: Booking a room in a hotel

3·1   1. b.   2. c.   3. a.

3·2   1. 2 people/4 nights/1 double   2. 5 people/8 nights/2 doubles and 1 single

3·3   1. Bom dia. Tem quartos vagos?   2. Para uma.   3. Para cinco.

4 Travel: A bus journey

4·1   2. Não, não é.   3. É sim.   4. Não, não é.

4·2   1. V   2. F   3. F

4·3   1. Leva dezassete minutos.   2. Leva treze minutos.   3. Leva dezanove minutos.

5 Directions: Getting to the tourist office

5·1   1. sim   2. não

5·2   Turn left, then straight ahead. Next, turn right and carry on, then turn right and the
tourist office is on the left of the square.

5·3   1. Desculpe, há um posto de Turismo aqui?   2. Fica muito longe?   3. Pode repetir mais
devagar, se faz favor?   4. Obrigado/a.

6 Town amenities: At the tourist office

6·1   1. c.   2. b.   3. a.

6·2   1. Braga/Monday   2. Oporto/Sunday

6·3   1. Bom dia.   2. Têm informações sobre o Porto?   3. Posso fazer reservas para
excursões aqui?   4. Para Fátima.   5. Queria dois bilhetes para a quarta-feira.

7 Downtown: Where can I . . .?

7·1 1. b. 2. d. 3. e. 4. a. 5. c.

7·2 1. bookshop in the square 2. butcher's on the corner, next to grocer's

7·3 1. Desculpe, onde é que posso comprar um livro? 2. Obrigada. Ah, outra coisa–onde é que posso comprar carne? 3. Obrigadinha.

8 Personal choices: Likes and dislikes

8·1 1. d. 2. a. 3. e. 4. b. 5. c.

8·2 José likes Braga, Lisboa, Albufeira. Ana likes Lisboa and Porto, but not Albufeira.

8·3 1. Gosto muito–há muito para ver. 2. Não, não gosto muito de Paris. 3. Sim, prefiro Madrid porque há muito para fazer.

9 Vacations: Discussing your holiday

9·1 2. O hotel é pequeno. 3. Os sapatos são bonitos. 4. As laranjas são baratas. 5. A camisa é cara.

9·2 Bom dia; cá; negócios; férias; férias; férias; é, não; caro; são; bonitas; visitar; ver; então.

9·3 1. Sim, estou. Gosto muito de Portugal. 2. Estou de férias, porque não faz tanto calor e é muito bonito. 3. Pretendo visitar Évora.

10 The weather: Talking about good weather

10·1 1. a. 2. e. 3. d. 4. c. 5. b.

10·2 Guarda–very hot, no wind, cloudy; Lisboa–good weather, blue sky, windy; Setúbal–not very hot; windy, cloudy, no blue sky.

10·3 1. Ainda bem! Queria cinco gelados, se faz favor. 2. Três sorvetes de morango e dois gelados. 3. Sim, o céu está azul e não há vento.

11 Ill health: Precautions in the sun

11·1 2. Este/This sky is blue. 3. Estes/These shoes are pretty. 4. Este/This man is good-looking. 5. Esta/This lady is fair. 6. Estes/These shoes are not expensive.

11·2 1. factor 10/twice a day 2. factor 16/once a day

11·3 1. Temos sim. Recomendo o fator número quinze. Precisa de usar três vezes por dia. 2. Temos sim. Recomendo o fator número doze. Precisa de usar uma vez por dia

12 Time: The best time for doing things

12·1 1. c. 2. a. 3. d. 4. b.

12·2 31, 62, 57, 92, 38, 49, 66, 55

12·3 1. Trinta e quatro minutos. 2. Sessenta e um minutos. 3. Noventa e sete minutos.

13 People: Getting to know people

13·1 1. English, German, French 2. Not French, Portuguese 3. German

13·2 1. German [2 check marks], Portuguese [one check mark] 2. French-, English-, German X 3. French [one check mark], German [one check mark], Portuguese [2 check marks] 4. French [2 check marks], English [one check mark], German X

13·3 1. Bom dia. Estou bem, obrigado/a. 2. E como está o senhor? 3. Obrigado/a. O senhor fala inglês? 4. Falo um pouco de alemão e também um pouco de francês.

14 Eating out: Making choices

14·1   1. é, fatia, bolo   2. a, com, sandes   3. pode, uma

14·2   1. V   2. F   3. F

14·3   1. Para mim, uma bica e uma fatia de bolo de chocolate.   2. O que tem de sanduíches?   3. Bom, para mim pode ser uma de ovo, se faz favor.

15 Accommodations: Reserving a room

15·1   1. c.   2. b.   3. d.   4. a

15·2   1. double room, with bath, with breakfast   2. single, with bath, no breakfast

15·3   1. Boa tarde, queria reservar um quarto de casal.   2. Para o dia vinte e sete de janeiro.   3. Duas. 4. Com, se faz favor.

16 Travel: A train journey

16·1   1. b.   2. d.   3. a.   4. e.   5. c

16·2   1. lst class   2. platform 8   3. 12 mins

16·3   1. Queria um bilhete de ida e volta para Braga, se faz favor.   2. Primeira.   3. Qual é a linha?

17 Directions: Finding out where the bank is

17·1   a. em frente do   b. na praça   c. detrás do d. ao lado do.

17·2   speaker 2

17·3   1. Onde fica o banco?   2. Desculpe, pode repetir mais devagar, se faz favor?   3. Fica longe? 4. Muito obrigada/o.

18 Town amenities: At the bank

18·1   1. f.   2. d.   3. a.   4. b.   5. c.   6. e.

18·2   6 cheques, £120, Sheraton, Rua Boavista 62, Lisboa.
2. Cinco, de vinte libras cada.

18·3   1. Queria trocar estes travellers cheques. 3. Aqui está.   4. Hotel Palácio, Rua Principal, número trinta e seis, Nazaré.

19 Downtown: Buying clothes at the shopping center

19·1   1. c.   2. a.   3. e.   4. b.   5. d.

19·2   Size 44; colors shown: blue, yellow, color chosen; blue.

19·3   1. Bom dia, queria comprar uma blusa.   2. É trinta e oito. Tem alguma coisa em verde?   3. Posso experimentar aquela?

20 Personal choices: When do you usually go shopping?

20·1   1. b.   2. d.   3. a.   4. c.   5. e.

20·2   José sometimes, often, sometimes. Paula: never, often, always.

20·3   1. Nem sempre, às vezes faço as compras no supermercado.   2 Quase nunca vou à feira.   3. Em geral, faço as compras lá nas quintas, mas esta semana ando muito ocupado.

21 Vacations: Where and when do you spend your holidays?

21·1   2. summer/Japan   3. spring/Germany   4. winter/Portugal   5. autumn/Switzerland

21·2   Greece, nowhere, England, Switzerland.

21·3   1. Passo as férias de primavera na França porque a paisagem é muito linda.   2. Nunca tiro férias no verão.   3. No outono gosto de visitar Portugal quando a costa está mais calma.

22 The weather: Talking about bad weather

22·1   1. b. 2. d. 3. a. 4. c. 5. e.

22·2   1. Cascais 2. Sagres

22·3   1. Que bom. Dois pacotes, se faz favor.   2. Tem razão, faz frio e o céu está nublado.   3. Às vezes, mas este ano há mais vento.   4. Hoje está um dia péssimo para a praia.

23 Ill health: Getting a cold

23·1   1. cabeça, c 2. garganta, a 3. constipada, b

23·2   male

23·3   1. Obrigado/a, estou constipado/a   2. Estou a tomar aspirina porque tenho uma dor de cabeça.   3. Boa ideia. Também tenho uma dor de garganta e estou muito cansado/a.

24 Time: Opening and closing times

24·1   1. d. 2. a. 3. c. 4. b. 5. e.

24·2   1. museum, 9:30 A.M., 6:40 P.M., 12–2:15   2. bakers, 7 A.M., 1:45 P.M., not mentioned

24·3   1. Abre às oito e vinte da manhã.   2. Fecha ao meio dia e meia para o almoço.   3. Depois, reabre à uma e um quarto.

25 People: Talking about families

25·1   1. a mulher 2. casados 3. o marido 4. a mãe 5. o pai 6. o filho
7. a filha 8. filhos 9. a irmã 10. o irmão

25·2   1. married, 2 children, no brothers; 2 sisters.   2. not married, no children, 3 brothers; 1 sister.

25·3   1. Ele fala inglês.   2. O senhor vive na Suécia?   3. Elas chamam-se Mary e Jean.   4. O irmão dele vive na França.   5. O marido dela chama-se José.

26 Eating out: Ordering a meal for two

26·1   1. c. 2. d. 3. b. 4. e. 5. a.

26·2   sopa de legumes, caldo verde, frango piri-piri, leitão, mousse de chocolate, gelado de baunilha, vinho branco.

26·3   1. A lista, se faz favor.   2. Para começar, um caldo verde e uma sopa de legumes.   3. Para mim, as sardinhas assadas e, para o meu irmão, o bacalhau.   4. O que tem?   5. Duas saladas de fruta.
6. Uma garrafa do vinho da casa.   7. Tinto, obrigado/a.

27 Accommodations: Checking into a campsite reservation

27·1   José, dos Santos Pereira; 25 de março de 1963; Castelo Branco, Rua S. Pedro, 10 3° esq. Braga, B1372201568BJL; Português, terça-feira, 10 de junho de 2010.

27·2   48 (T.)

27·3   (your name), (your surname), (your date of birth), (your place of birth), (your address), (your passport number), (your nationality)

28 Travel: A coach journey

28·1   b. quinze   c. Lisboa   d. Braga

28·2   Albufeira, every 20 min; 10.35, direct, 12.40.

28·3   1. A que horas há uma camioneta para Viana? Response: Every 20 minutes (de 20 em 20 minutos.)
2. É direta? Response: Yes it is (Sim, é.)

29 Directions: Getting to the right platform

29·1   1. b.   2. d.   3. a.   4. c.   5. e.

29·2   Directions: turn right, pass in front of ticket office, go up to steps. Go up and over footbridge. Descend and turn right. Platform for France is the second one along Platform number 8.

29·3   1. O comboio para Braga sai de que linha?   2. E para chegar lá?   3. Espere um momento, já estou perdido/a!   4. O senhor é muito gentil, obrigado/a.

30 Town amenities: At the post office

30·1   1. b.   2. d.   3. a.   4. c.   5. e.

30·2   Spain, 2205, 75288, sr González

30·3   Queria fazer uma chamada a cobrar no destino. (country) (town code) (phone number) (name of person you want to talk to) (your name)

31 Downtown: Shopping at the market

31·1   1. c.   2. a.   3. d.   4. b.   5. e.

31·2   They buy: 2 kg pears, 2 cauliflowers, 250g mushrooms, 3 kg potatoes, 1 kg oranges, 1/2 kg tomatoes. Not available today: lettuce.

31·3   1. Bom dia. Tem cogumelos hoje?   2. Dê-me/queria duzentos e cinquenta gramas.   3. Também queria meio quilo de peras, três alfaces, e seis quilos de batatas.   4. Tem melão?   5. Então dê-me um quilo de maçãs.   6. A como é a laranja hoje?   7. Dê-me dois quilos, obrigado/a.

32 Personal choices: What would you like to do?

32·1   1. cinema/ver   2. bar/tomamos   3. jantar   4. ir/museu   5. passar/boate

32·2   Eduardo prefers on Saturday: relax in bar, eat in, go dancing; on Sunday: see film. Paula prefers on Saturday: see film, stroll in centre; on Sunday: eat out, relax in bar.

32·3   1. Gostaria de tomar uma bebida num bar   2. Preferia jantar fora   3. Não, preferia ir ver um filme.

33 Vacations: Discussing next year's holidays

33·1   1. vamos/visitar/no ano que vem   2. (ela) vai/ficar/na semana que vem   3. no mês que vem/vais/ver
4. vou/viajar/no ano que vem   5. na semana que vem/(eles.) vão/passear

33·2   1. next week/see a friend/Holland   2. next month/pottery course/library

33·3   1. No ano que vem eu e a minha família vamos visitar a Dinamarca no inverno.   2. Onde vai passar as férias no mês que vem?   3. No mês que vem vou ficar em casa e fazer um curso de português.

34 The weather: Weather reports

34·1   1. F   2. V   3. F   4. F   5. V

34·2   Madrid 12°; London 3°; Paris 8°; Amsterdam 0°; Rome 14°

34·3   1. Boa noite, aqui temos a previsão do tempo para hoje para Inglaterra.   2. Na região do norte, o céu vai estar nublado com vento moderado.   3. As temperaturas vão chegar a dezoito graus no sul.
4. A qualidade do ar observada em Londres é razoável.

35 Ill health: Feeling ill

35·1 1. arm   2. foot   3. eyes   4. stomach   5. teeth

35·2 has pain in legs and head, has hurt back

35·3 1. Bom dia. Não me sinto muito bem.   2. Tenho uma dor de cabeça e doem-me os dentes.
3. Ontem magoei a cabeça e cortei o dedo.   4. Nos olhos, não, mas dói-me o estômago.

36 Time: Discussing when things happened

36·1 1. d.   2. c.   3. a.   4. e.   5. b.

36·2 1. 8:15   2. 12:00   3. 7:00   4. 11:10

36·3 1. Ontem de manhã fui para o trabalho cedo e voltei a casa para almoçar à uma e meia.   2. Depois, saí para ir à biblioteca.   3. Fui a um restaurante com um amigo.   4. Comi frango, bolo de amêndoa, e bebi meia garrafa de vinho branco.   5. Eram onze e um quarto quando cheguei em casa.

37 People: Discussing jobs and professions

37·1 1. c.   2. a.   3. d.   4. e.

37·2 1. José; designer; doesn't mention   2. Ana Maria; doesn't mention, school   3. Paulo; civil servant; Lisbon.

37·3 1. Boa tarde, Teresa.   2. Sou desenhador. Trabalho numa empresa internacional em Lisboa.
3. Sim, gosto muito.   4. A minha mulher trabalha numa escola. É secretária.   5. O que é que faz, Teresa?

38 Eating out: Asking about what's on the menu

38·1 queríamos, salada, meia-dose, arroz, traga, sobremesa, fruta, cafés.

38·2 Dish 1 has cod, garlic, carrots, olives, tomato, rice; Dish 2 has pork, garlic, rice, onion, green pepper, olives. Joan can eat dish no. 2.

38·3 1. Sim, queríamos o bacalhau na cataplana e uma feijoada.   2. Meia dose dá para uma pessoa?Então, só meia dose do bacalhau.   4. Os pratos vêm com batatas fritas ou salada?   5. Então, traga uma salada também, por favor.

39 Accommodations: Inside a house

39·1 1. e.   2. b.   3. a.   4. d.   5. f.   6. e.

39·2 1. sala de estar   2. cozinha   3. jardim   4. quarto   5. casa de banho   6. W.C.

39·3 1. os meus quartos   2. a tua casa   3. o seu jardim   4. as suas cozinhas   5. a sala de estar dele
6. a sala de jantar dela

40 Travel: A visit to a petrol/gasoline station

40·1 1. e.   2. f.   3. d.   4. a.   5. c.

40·2 1. 4-star fill tank; 5 liters oil   2. 20 liters diesel; ½ liter oil

40·3 1. Bom dia. Enche o depósito, se faz favor.   2. Normal sem chumbo, se faz favor.   3. Tem óleo?
4. Dois litros.   5. Vendem mapas da região?   6. Está bem. Obrigada/o. Adeus.

41 Directions: Traveling by car

41·1 1. b.   2. d.   3. a.   4. c.   5. e.

41·2 Lisboa; no; left at lights; 200 km.

41·3 1. Para Viseu? Não é por aqui.   2. Tem que voltar para trás até aos semáforos, e depois virar à esquerda e tomar a estrada para Guarda.   3. Logo vai ver uma rotunda, –é só seguir o sinal que diz Viseu, e pronto, chegará.   4. Sim, é um pouco longe. Viseu fica a uns noventa e cinco quilómetros daqui.

42 Town amenities: Sports and leisure facilities

42·1 desportos; piscina; hípico; cavalo; campo; ténis; sócio; jogar; piquenique; parque.

42·2 swimming; park; football; golf course; picnic areas.

42·3 1. Bom dia. Tem informações sobre os desportos na cidade?   2. A piscina abre todos os dias?
3. Tem que ser sócio para jogar golfe?   4. Onde fica o campô de golfe?   5. Obrigado/a

43 Downtown: Shopping for souvenirs

43·1 1. preto   2. vermelhas   3. lindos   4. pesados   5. nacional

43·2 cockerel: yes, red, orange, white; tablecloths: yes; white, orange; tiles; yes; not specified; tile panels; yes; not specified; shawl: no.

43·3 1. Bom dia. Estou à procura duma lembrança típica de Portugal para a minha filha. O que recomenda?
2. Tem xailes pretos?   3. Tem azulejos?   4. Não quero nada muito pesado.   5. Boa ideia. Também vou levar um xaile preto.

44 Personal choices: Talking about sports and hobbies

44·1 nadar/ler/pintar/andar/ouvir música

44·2 1. likes golf, swimming, indoor activities like reading; dislikes music   2. likes painting, sports, likes golf; dislikes bike riding

44·3 1. Gosto de andar de bicicleta e de nadar.   2. A bicicleta,   3. Às vezes gosto de ouvir música,
4. O meu marido gosta de ler. Detesta os desportos.

45 Vacations: Discussing last year's holidays

45·1 1. c.   2. f.   3. a.   4. d.   5. e.   6. b.

45·2 1. Italy; husband; liked; Rome.   2. France; didn't like; south and Paris.   3. Brazil; Pedro; liked; Rio.

45·3 1. O ano passado fui à Madeira com a minha família.   2. Gostámos muito, mas a minha mulher não gostou da comida.   3. Sim, visitámos Funchal e vimos as levadas.   4. Sim, mas também foi um pouco cansativo.

46 The weather: Talking about climates

46·1 1. V   2. F   3. F   4. F   5. V

46·2 Winter; N. hot; S. quite cold; E. not mentioned; W. more rain. Summer; N. tropical, hot, lots of rain; S. less hot, dry; E. humid, hot; W. very dry.

46·3 1. Nem sempre Maria. O nosso clima cá é bastante variável.   2. No inverno é frio no norte, e chove muito.   3. No verão é quente no sul, e bastante quente no norte.   4. É um pouco, mas o clima em Portugal na primavera e no verão é melhor.   5. Não gosto dum clima demasiado quente, então o clima da Grã-Bretanha é perfeito para mim.

47 Ill health: A trip to the hospital

47·1 1. um tornozelo partido.   2. um médico.   3. gesso.   4. uma radiografia.   5. um pulso inchado.

47·2 1. knee; broken; yes; 7 weeks; yes; 2 months.   2. ankle; twisted; no; yes; 5 weeks.

47·3 1. Preciso de ver um médico, por favor.   2. Penso que tenho um tornozelo partido.   3. Hoje de manhã fui atropelada por uma bicicleta.   4. Vou ter que descansar?

48 Time: Asking the time

48·1 1. d.   2. b.   3. e.   4. a.   5. c.

48·2 1. 4:40; bookshop; – ; 5 P.M.   2. 12:30; baker's; – ; 2 P.M.   3. 7:15; butcher's; 8 A.M.; – .

48·3 1. Que horas são, Sandra? 2. Bom, ainda chegamos a tempo. 3. Às três horas. 4. Sim, mas ainda temos que achar um lugar onde estacionar o carro. 5. Chegámos mesmo à hora, vamos entrar.

49 People: Talking about age

49·1 1. c. 2. a. 3. d. 4. b. 5. e.

49·2 1. Aunt; 46 2. Grandpa; 72 3. Grandson; 9

49·3 1. Paulo, venha conhecer os meus filhos. 2. David, que é o mais velho, tem dezasseis anos e Laura, que é mais nova, tem catorze. 3. David faz anos no dia vinte e cinco de março e Laura fez anos a semana passada. 4. Faço anos no dia três de novembro.

50 Eating out: Making a complaint

50·1 1. b. 2. e. 3. a. 4. d. 5. g.

50·2 1. spoon; missing 2. bill; wrong 3. glass; dirty

50·3 1. Faz favor. 2. Faltam duas facas, e este garfo está sujo. Pode trazer outros? 3. Outra coisa, o peru não está bom, e este copo está rachado.

51 Accommodations: When things don't work

51·1 1. frigorífico 2. condicionado 3. água 4. fecha 5. chuveiro 6. comida

51·2 1. air conditioning; tap 2. shower

51·3 1. Não tenho nenhuma. 2. Não tem nenhum. 3. Não, ninguém fala. 4. Não têm nenhuma.

52 Travel: Air travel

52·1 passaporte; aqui; quer; malas; só; e; vou; está bem; Itália; trinta e cinco minutos; porta; quinze.

52·2 1. AF365/Paris/yes/50 mins/12 2. 1B236/Madrid/no/-/22 3. RG558/Brazil/yes/25 mins/6

52·3 1. Tem passaporte e bilhete, senhor? 2. Quer passar a sua mala à balança. 3. Só tem esta? 4. O voo TAP567 para Faro vai ter um atraso de 20 minutos. 5. Pode passar para a porta número catorze.

53 Directions: Getting around the airport

53·1 1. comprar 2. vinho 3. carrinho 4. pagar 5. fazer 6. dinheiro

53·2 1. car hire/through here, turn right 2. baggage reclaim/through here, straight ahead, near customs

53·3 1. Claro. A senhora passa por ali, em frente, vira à esquerda, e vai ver o aluguer de carros mesmo em frente. 2. Claro. É só virar aqui à direita e, ao chegar à alfândega, vai ver os lavabos à esquerda. 3. De nada.

54 Town amenities: Buying bus tickets at the kiosk

54·1 1. Um euro e vinte cêntimos 2. Três euros 3. Sessenta cêntimos 4. Quatro euros e vinte cêntimos 5. Um euro e oitenta cêntimos

54·2 1. a. 2. a. 3. b.

54·3 1. Bom dia. Quanto custa um bilhete de autocarro para a Baixa? 2. Pode-se usar nos elétricos? 3. Então, queria seis, se faz favor.

55 Downtown: Buying groceries

55·1 quilo; ovos; garrafão; sal; pouco; queijo.

55·2 Ana forgets 1 kg flour.

55·3 1. Bom dia, Sr. Silva. Preciso dumas coisas.   2. Quero um quilo de farinha e trezentos gramas de chouriço.   3. Sim, também quero meio quilo de açúcar.   4. Uma dúzia de ovos e um pacote de manteiga.   5. É tudo, obrigada.

56 Personal choices: Favorite modes of transportation

56·1 1. b. confortável   2. d. rápido   3. a. lento   4. c. caro   5. e. eficiente

56·2 1. plane–very quick/boat–I feel sick.   2. car–comfortable/on foot–too slow.

56·3 1. Adoro. É confortável e barato.   2. Não, acho o avião demasiado caro para mim.   3. Às vezes vou de autocarro ou, às vezes, a pé.   4. Não gosto de viajar de moto–é rápido demais para mim.

57 Vacations: Talking about a cultural holiday/vacation

57·1 1. fui   2. passou   3. visitaram   4. gostaste   5. viu

57·2 1. castle; last week; 2 hours   2. city, art exhibition; last Sunday; 55 mins   3. botanical gardens; yesterday; 3 ½ hours

57·3 1. Fui a Londres e passei a semana a fazer coisas culturais.   2. Sim, fui. Havia uma exposição de pinturas do século dezasseis.   3. Só passei duas horas lá. Não houve tempo para fazer tudo.   4. Sim, há tantas coisas para fazer.

58 The weather: Talking about yesterday's weather

58·1 1. c.   2. a.   3. d.   4. b.   5. e.

58·2 1. Tuesday; very windy, rain   2. Saturday; very bad, thunder, lightning, lot of rain

58·3 1. Eu sei. Não pude sair. Havia muito vento.   2. Creio que hoje vamos ter geada.   3. Quem me dera viver num país tropical!

59 Ill health: Dealing with an accident

59·1 1. V3   2. F3   3. F3   4. V   5. F

59·2 Rua Principal; 4; Ana Mendes; Liberdade Chemist.

59·3 1. Houve um acidente, precisamos duma ambulância,   2. Na esquina da Rua da Sé com a Rua do Brasil. Há cinco pessoas feridas.   3. Chamo-me (your name.).   4. A Farmácia Mendes. Venha depressa, por favor.

60 Time: Departure and arrival times

60·1 1. o barco; dez e quinze   2. o avião; vinte e uma e vinte/nove e vinte   3. O autocarro/o ônibus; três e quarenta   4. o táxi; oito e treze   5. O comboio/o trem; dezassete e cinquenta/cinco e cinquenta

60·2 boat; 19:20; yes; 30 mins; rain; 05:35 2. plane; 08:10; no;–;–; 11:35

60·3 1. O próximo barco para o Brasil partirá às dez e vinte.   2. Houve um atraso de duas horas por causa do mau tempo.   3. Provavelmente o barco chegará na quinta-feira às oito e trinta.   4. Já fez o check-in?   5. Então pode passar para a sala de espera.

Language and topic indexes

Numbers refer to units.

Language

Topics